WILLIAM HENRY BELK

WILLIAM HENRY BELK

WILLIAM
HENRY
BELK

Merchant of the South

BY

LeGETTE BLYTHE

Chapel Hill

THE UNIVERSITY OF NORTH CAROLINA PRESS

TO THE MEMORY

OF A NOBLE WOMAN

SARAH WALKUP BELK SIMPSON

FOREWORD

By John J. Parker

UNITED STATES CIRCUIT COURT OF APPEALS

When I recall the names of those to whom I feel deeply indebted for the assistance they have given me in life, Mr. Henry Belk and his brother, Dr. John M. Belk, occupy a prominent place on the list. I feel indebted to them, not merely because they gave me employment when I needed it and thus enabled me to earn the money with which I began my collegiate education, but chiefly because they instilled sound and correct business ideas and principles into my youthful mind. They reinforced by example and by precept the lesson which I had been taught at home that personal character is the only safe foundation upon which to build. The wages paid me for my work, although they seem meager now, were tremendously important to me then; but infinitely more important than the wages, although I did not realize it then, was the opportunity of beginning my life's work in the wholesome atmosphere created by two honest men who believed in God and entertained a spirit of good will toward those who were struggling along with them amid the hard conditions of that far-off day.

Mr. Henry Belk is a great merchant and businessman. Beginning as an humble helper in a country store while the dark shadows of war and Reconstruction still hung like a pall over our Southland, at a monthly wage less than a skilled mechanic now demands for half a day's work and with nothing but his high character and the inspiration of a Godly mother to help him, he worked hard, made friends, and saved from his meager wages until he had accumulated a few hundred dollars. With this and a few hundred more that he was able to borrow, he bought a small stock of goods from a failing neighbor and launched into business for himself. From then on the record of his life reads like an Alger success story or a tale from the Arabian Nights. The little store in Monroe grew and other stores were added. The simple merchandising of the country town became a complicated commercial system of nearly three hundred stores extending over the entire South. The pitiful savings of the hard-working clerk grew into many millions of dollars. Success of this sort cannot be shrugged off or discounted. It comes only where there is real ability at its foundation.

It is not in the making of money, however, that the life of Mr. Belk is most significant. After all, many other men have made more than he. What he has accomplished is significant in that it affords fine illustration of the application of the democratic principle in the realm of business. All of the Belk stores are like great families in which the personality of even the humblest helper is respected and in which the ideal of service to the public is never forgotten. Infinitely more important than the accumulation of his fortune is what Mr. Belk has done for hundreds of men and women in furnishing them employment in the atmosphere of an honest and friendly business and the opportunity which he has afforded the especially talented among his employees to launch a business for themselves. The Belk stores are not a chain dominated and exploited for a single individual or group of stockholders. Each store is a separate undertaking headed by some man who as a youth has been set up in business by Mr. Belk as a partner in the undertaking. Many of the problems of American business would vanish if the principles of friendliness and fair dealing which Mr. Belk has followed could be generally applied.

Mr. LeGette Blythe has written an interesting account of the life of this remarkable man and of his rise in the world. It is more than a biography. It is a true picture of the life of the South as it was recovering from the horrors of war and Reconstruction. It is more even than this. It is indisputable proof of the value of our system of free enterprise and a vivid demonstration of the copybook maxims of an earlier day which too many of us have been prone to forget. No more graphic illustration can be found that "Industry, honesty and economy generally insure success," nor a more striking example of the truth of the ancient proverb, "Seest thou a man diligent in his business? He shall stand before kings. He shall not stand before mean men."

Charlotte, North Carolina
February 1, 1950

PREFACE

William Henry Belk: Merchant of the South was originally published by the University of North Carolina Press on June 2, 1950, Mr. Belk's eighty-eighth birth anniversary.

Less than two years later, on February 21, 1952, Mr. Belk died. Some months afterward it was agreed by members of the Belk family and business associates, the publisher, and the author that a second edition should be prepared and published that would complete the life story of the noted Southern merchant and philanthropist.

It was determined that it would be best to incorporate into the new book the first edition substantially as it was published, with the addition to it of material summarizing that part of his life not covered in the original edition, his death, and selected editorials and articles appraising his long life of achievement.

This plan was followed. Certain brief material, however, was added in the chapters of the first edition and errors in that book were corrected, Belk stores established since the release of the first volume were added to the chronological list, and a revised index was provided.

The author is unwilling to close this explanatory note without paying his affectionate personal tribute to "Mr. Henry" and expressing his happiness in having been afforded the good fortune of knowing well this humble and unassuming, but great and good, man of our beloved Southland.

Huntersville, North Carolina
June 30, 1957

CONTENTS

ILLUSTRATIONS

I

THE SOIL

1

ACROSS MORE THAN FOUR-FIFTHS OF A CENTURY OF IN-
credible change William Henry Belk remembers the day his
father left home to escape the advancing Federals. It was
1865, and the Confederacy was dragging wearily into its last
days.

The cause for which the reckless, singing young men had
gone off to battle and to die, for which countless young wives
and mothers had toiled along furrows and beside spinning
frames, was soon to become the lost cause. The South was
almost prostrate now; even Sarah Walkup Belk's beloved

Waxhaw country, the country of Andrew Jackson, the gallant William Richardson Davie, and her own Wauchope family, lay under the heel and the torch of Sherman. This federal general, whose very name throughout the South provoked terror and wrath, was moving north after his march to the sea, pillaging and burning and slaughtering, and in the path of his troops, in the border region between South Carolina and North Carolina, lay the modest home of Abel Nelson Washington Belk. If young Belk, whose weak lungs had prevented his joining the Confederate Army, should be found at home, the Belks feared that Sherman's men would steal his property, burn the house, and possibly hang him. If he should leave and hide out with some of the Negroes and the valuables that could be moved, the marauding Yankees might spare the house. Perhaps even Sherman's men might not be willing to have a house burned down over the heads of a defenseless young woman and her three babies.

Henry Belk was the younger of the two little boys who held to Sarah Walkup Belk's skirt that dismal morning in the early spring of 1865 as the man of the family walked out of their home and out of their lives. Thomas Milburn Belk, named for his father's father, was four years and four months old. John Montgomery Belk, named for his mother's mother's father, was seven months. Henry was two years and eight months old, but he recalls vividly his father and the Negroes leaving with the teams. Countless times he has repeated the story, always in its barest outline, devoid of coloring details, always starkly dramatic:

"My father had heard that old Sherman was heading our way on his march towards Charlotte. He had what in those days they called weak lungs, and he hadn't been strong enough to join the Confederate Army.

"He figured that if the Yankees came along by our place and caught him at home, they'd probably hang him and take all the horses and anything else they wanted, and burn down the house. He thought that if he'd hide out, maybe they'd spare the house. So he loaded up the wagons and took some of the Negroes and they went down on Gill's Creek some fifteen miles from our home and six or seven miles east of Lancaster, South Carolina, on the road from Lancaster to Chesterfield Courthouse. That was pretty close to his father's home. He figured on refugeeing on the creek down there until the Yankees had got out of the country.

"Old man Tom Belk—that was my grandfather—had the name of being rich. He was the big man down in that part of the country. He had been working slaves in his gold mine and a lot of people thought he had plenty of gold hid out.

"But old Sherman's men didn't come by our house. Because of some unexpected resistance they had run into they turned off the Charlotte road and went down the way my grandfather lived. And it wasn't long before the Yankees caught a fellow down that way who figured he'd save his own hide and get in their good graces by turning up my grandfather, old man Tom Belk. This scoundrel told them that my grandfather had barrels of gold hid out at his mine and he said that if they caught him they could make him tell where the gold was.

"But the Yankees made a mistake and caught my father instead of my grandfather. They asked him where the gold was hid out. He told them he didn't know. But they thought he was just trying to save his gold. So they took him down to the creek—we heard all this later—and held him by the feet and pushed his head down under the water. Then they'd jerk him up and ask him again where the gold was. When he'd tell them he didn't know—which he didn't—they'd push him down again. That went on several times.

" 'I can't stand it,' my father told them. 'You're going to drown me.' But they kept on dousing him under the water.

They were determined to make him tell where the gold was hid out.

" 'I just can't stand it,' my father kept telling them. But they just wouldn't listen. They kept on sticking his head under the water.

"His weak lungs couldn't stand it. I reckon they just filled with water. I guess those Yankees thought he would finally tell them where the gold was. They didn't know that he really didn't know where it was, I guess. I reckon they didn't mean to drown him—don't reckon they cared much one way or the other.

"But they did drown him. I don't remember anything about that, of course, except what I have been told. But I do remember seeing him going down the hill with the Negroes and the wagons that day he left home to refugee on Gill's Creek."

A letter which was written by Henry Belk's uncle to Sarah Walkup Belk was her first news of the tragedy. It read as follows:

March 8th 1865,
Sister Sarah, I have sad news to tell you. Abel, your husband and my brother, is I suppose no more. He is not found as we know but there was a certain person buried about one and a half miles below here, in Graham's field, who I suppose is Abel.

Ely tells us that the man had shoes on with iron heels and iron on the toes of his shoes, like those Abel had on. His clothes were like those Abel had on. He had whiskers on his upper lip. He had light colored hair like Brother Abel and someone told Ely that he was about as tall as I am.

The man was found in the creek not far from Gill's Creek Church and was supposed to have been drowned near to, or a little below a pine log which was across the creek.

Dear Sister Sarah, I know that you will be extremely sorry to receive such sad news from me, but I still have some hope that it is not Abel who was found dead, though Abel's little mule is lying dead in the road not far from where the man was drowned.

Brother Abel was with us for several days. He was sick and had chills Saturday. He was with Father on Sunday, separated from Father Sunday morning.

Ely said that Abel left him and Ben at Preacher Brasington's about 10 O'Clock Sunday. This is the last we have heard from him.

Well dear Sarah, I propose for you and your friends to come first to my house on Friday night. I will circulate word among the neighbors to come and we will raise the man that was buried in Graham's field early Saturday morning and if it be Brother Abel, we will have him taken and buried at Shiloh Church.

Sister Sarah you must bring horses and gears to haul him to Shiloh graveyard for burial as we have not a team of horses. The Yankees have taken our horses.

Sister Sarah do not grieve too much for our kind Brother and your dear Husband for he may yet be alive.

Come to my house Friday night for we cannot raise him before then. Circulate the word to Father, Kitchen and others.

Herron.

It was a cheerless, somber day when Sarah Walkup Belk turned away from the red mound in old Shiloh graveyard. But even darker were the thoughts that threatened to crush her, for everywhere she seemed to sense the very presence of death. Beyond the stones of the graveyard, many of them already beginning to crumble with great age, lay fields bare and brown and dead, and there was little promise anywhere that the resurrection of spring would provide adequate crops. The Confederacy, too, she knew, was at its death and tired hungry hopeless men could no longer stem the rush of advancing hordes from the north. And now her husband was dead. What should she do now? Where should she turn? How could she make a living for herself and her three babies? How actually find enough food? Sometimes it seemed that doubt and despair would engulf her. Sometimes the gloom appeared almost impenetrable. But never entirely. Always when the darkness was heaviest the pinpoint of a star broke through. She held to her faith. And she worked.

She went back to her farm and organized what poor efforts she could command. She found food and clothing for herself, her babies, and the Negroes. She managed to provide security in those perilous days, joy even and much love. And always she taught her children. When the days were darkest she would repeat over and over again and in staunch faith the prayer and the prophecy of that day when without knowing it she had waved her last good-bye to her young husband: "God will protect us; God will take care of us."

2

THE YEAR OF ABEL NELSON WASHINGTON BELK'S TRAGIC
death brought also the death of southern hopes. The Waxhaw
country, and all the land that had given allegiance to the
cause of the South, was prostrate. Its economy was shattered,
the finest of its youth was slaughtered. Nothing remained
but hope and courage, and often hope all but fled like the
thin vagary of a vanished dream.

But courage stayed, and faith. From the quiet graveyard
of old Shiloh Church, Sarah Walkup Belk had gone back to
the small house upon the crest of the rise. With the scant re-

sources now available and the few farmhands she was able to obtain, she produced a crop that first year and prayed earnestly for a more secure future.

The slaves had been freed. Few of them knew what to do with their freedom, and others professed they did not want it. They were leaderless children looking for their way in a new land and a strange day. For them Sarah Belk, as well as most other enlightened former slave owners, felt a responsibility and considerable affection. So when some of these freedmen and their wives came to Mrs. Belk seeking employment, she entered into a formal agreement with them.

This agreement survives as an interesting and highly enlightening document revealing the times and the people of the Waxhaws and the South generally. It is entitled: "Sarah N. Belk Enters into an Agreement with Former Slaves. South Carolina, Lancaster District, Jan. 17th, 1866."

The document begins:

"Know all men by these presents, that I, Sarah N. Belk, of the district, and the state aforesaid, have this day entered into an agreement with the following freedmen, for the year 1866: Alexander, Ely, and Ben. Alexander and Ben, each having a wife and child, do agree that their wives be represented as one hand; the five making four hands in the crop. I, Sarah N. Belk, am to find land, horses and horse feed; and bear half the expenses of the ploughs and tools necessary for working the farm.

"I, Sarah N. Belk, do herein set forth, that I must have a white man to work with the above named freedmen and women, and he is to receive an equal portion with them, of their half of the crop.

"We, and each of us, to wit—Alexander, Ely, and Ben, do, hereby, set forth, that we are to furnish our own provisions and clothing for ourselves and our families, and bear an equal expense of the corn and cotton seed necessary for planting the crop, with the exception of the white man's part."

Next follow the obligations of the former slaves:

"We, Alexander, Ely, and Ben; and Amanda, the wife of Ben; and Moriah, the wife of Alexander, do hereby, obligate ourselves to give attention, and labor exclusively to the plantation; rising early, feeding the stock, and being ready for work by sunrise, working throughout the day, except one hour and a half at twelve o'clock, and working six days in each week, except one-half of every other Saturday.

"The said freedmen and women do, hereby, bind themselves to take good care of all the stock, and property belonging to the plantation, and if any of the property or stock be injured by carelessness or negligence, by any of the above named freedmen or women, he or she will make the full compensation for the loss, which will be deducted out of the crop.

"We, Alexander, Ely, Ben, Amanda, and Moriah, do, herein, bind ourselves to attend to the wants of Sarah N. Belk, and she is privileged to use the horses at any time she deems it necessary."

But in the agreement Mrs. Belk promises not to take advantage of the clause permitting her the use of the horses:

"I, Sarah N. Belk, do, herein, say that I will not take the horses unnecessarily, in work time from the crop, neither shall others have them when needed for the farm.

"We, to wit, Alexander, Ely, and Ben, representing, also our wives, do obligate ourselves to purchase all of our provisions from Sarah N. Belk, or if we do get things from others we are first to inform her of it, and get her consent, otherwise the above named freedmen or women are not to buy or bring any provisions on the place."

"We, Alexander, Ely, Ben, Amanda, and Moriah, furthermore, agree to follow the dictates of Sarah N. Belk, or those of anyone that she might have to attend to her affairs.

"We, Alexander, and Ben, also, set forth that we are willing that our wives assist Sarah N. Belk in her domestic affairs, and we, Amanda and Moriah do obligate ourselves to assist alternately, the said Sarah N. Belk in cooking, milking, and washing, etc."

Here the document becomes general:

"It is, also, set forth, herein, that the above named freedmen must pay their own Doctor bills for themselves and families, and that any time lost by sickness or otherwise unnecessarily, shall be kept account of, and reduction from their part of the crop shall be taken in accordance therewith, and be added to those who work the most.

"In case all the above named freedmen or women, or either of them, do not comply with the obligations and requisitions, herein, set forth, I, Sarah N. Belk, reserve the right to discharge them from the place uncompensated, and will be privileged to procure others in their place.

"The indebtedness for provisions and other necessities purchased from Sarah N. Belk, shall be paid out of the crop by the above named freedmen or women before it shall be removed from the place.

"We, the above named freedmen and women, do also, herein, obligate ourselves to do any work on the plantation deemed necessary for its improvement, that might be required of them by Sarah N. Belk, or anyone that she might have employed.

"Witness, whereof, we do set our hands and seals."

Sarah N. Belk signed her name. Alexander, Ben, Ely, Amanda, and Moriah made their marks.

Out of necessity Sarah Narcissus Walkup Belk had become the head of the house; out of the great admiration and affection of her children she remained its head until her death on March 9, 1932.

3

ON A WARM SPRING AFTERNOON IN 1948 WILLIAM HENRY
Belk rode in a long black automobile up the slope down
which his father had ridden in a creaking wagon on a cold
day in early spring eighty-three years before.

"This isn't the house we lived in," he said, when the car
reached the crest. "That house was torn down. But this is the
place; it stood right there. My father went off down that way
the morning he started out to refugee on Gill's Creek. I just
can remember seeing him as he went off with the Negroes.
That was a long time ago. I wasn't quite three. But I can remember that morning."

The car slowly circled the house, started down the hill. "I bought the old place," said Mr. Belk. "Don't reckon I had much need for it, but I just wanted to own it. I've got a good deal of land down in this community, a lot of it owned by my folks away back. I don't think I'm making much out of it—" He grinned, hesitated. "My wife claims I'm going in the hole. But I just like to own it."

Half an hour later the car was purring along a sand-clay, back-country South Carolina road. For a while in silence Mr. Belk watched the red acres roll past the car windows. Then he turned to his guests in the rear seat. "The Belks and the Wauchopes have been living in this country a long time," he said. "They say the first Belk in this part of the country was old man John Belk, who came over from England about two hundred years ago. He was the daddy of the family in this part of the country. He took up a lot of land grants in this section and some over in Johnston County in North Carolina and settled in what is now Mecklenburg—back in those days it was still Anson County. Old man John Belk must have liked to own land, too; the old deeds show that he owned a lot of it. Maybe that's where I got my liking for land.

"The Belks are English and the Wauchopes are Scotch," he went on. "They call themselves Scotch-Irish in this section, because their forefathers came over to the north of Ireland from Scotland so they could be free to worship the way they wanted to. Then from Ireland they came on over to America. They didn't mix much with the Irish while they were in Ireland; I understand they were pretty straight-out Scotch, and strong Presbyterians."

John Belk, the grandfather of Mr. Belk's grandfather to whom he had referred, evidently did get much satisfaction out of acquiring land, judging by the records which substantiate Mr. Belk's conclusion. Grants recorded in the Land Grant Office, Department of State, State of North Carolina, in Raleigh, show large tracts in his name in Johnston, Lincoln, and Mecklenburg counties entered between the years 1762 and 1798. A Johnston County grant lists "300 Acres granted May 21, 1762, Located on the North side of Crab Tree." A Lincoln County grant was for "30 Acres, granted Nov. 27, 1792, Located on Dutchman's Creek. Signed by Alex. Martin." An entry records a grant of "200 Acres, granted Nov. 26, 1789, Located on the Pole Catt branch. Signed by Sam. Johnston," in Mecklenburg County. Another record lists a grant to Belk of "110 Acres, granted April 12, 1798, lying on the waters of Buffalo—a branch of Lincheys Creek. Signed by Samuel Ashe." Still another Mecklenburg grant was for "200 acres, granted April 12, 1798, located on the waters of Linches Creek. Signed by Samuel Ashe."

A transaction recorded in Mecklenburg County Courthouse and dated September 25, 1783, reveals that "James Belk, for 20 pds. specie, sold to John Belk, Sr., 100 Acres of Land, in Mecklenburg Co., North fork of Lynches Creek." The witness signed his name: "Darlin Belk." Both James and Darling Belk were sons of John Belk, Sr.

Still another sale, recorded also in Mecklenburg, was that of "William Shepherd and wife, Jamiah, of Anson Co." to "John Belk, Sr., of Anson Co., 100 acres of land lying on Strouds Fork of Lynches Creek, for the sum of 100 pds." The witness was James Belk and the deed was dated October 6, 1778.

John Belk accumulated much money and land and many slaves, as evidenced by his will, dated July 20, 1804, and recorded in the Mecklenburg Courthouse. Bequests to various children and grandchildren of "silver dollars" and "pounds" indicate he was a man of considerable affluence for that day and region. Bringing alive the days of the past are such items in the will as "I leave my son, John Belk, my negro fellow, Brick, and his wife, Sylvia," and "I leave to my son,

Darling Belk, one negro girl named Tillar, and one negro girl named Hager. And the first child that Tillar has I leave to my grand-daughter, Sara Belk, daughter of Darling Belk." And another: "I also will that Rose and her children be left with my wife during her life or widow-hood and I leave old Dick on my plantation and devise that he be taken care of."

Family records list seven children of John Belk. They were John, Darling, James, Britain (whose name is variously given also as Britian, Britton, and Brittain) and three daughters, Nisey, Francis (spelled with an i) and Gracey. The son John was married twice, the second time to Hannah Nelson, and their son Thomas Milburn Belk was Abel Nelson Washington Belk's father.

"They must have been English, all right," Mr. Belk observed that afternoon as he talked of his forebears on his father's side. "My grandfather named all of his children three names, as the English customarily do. My father's name was Abel Nelson Washington Belk. It was too long to handle very well."

So were the names of the others, all eight of them. His nine children were: John Thomas Milburn, Jr., Joab Grandison Mushatt (or Machette), James Thomas Kitchen, William Robert Herron, Dickey Darling Anderson, Mary Hannah Lucinda, Abel Nelson Washington, Milly Agnes Matilda, and Josiah Montgomery Dixon.

"It's a wonder," commented Mr. Belk, after he had enumerated them, "that my grandfather didn't run out of names before the children stopped coming."

After a while the car climbed another slight slope and stopped before a large farmhouse. "This is where Captain James Wauchope lived," Mr. Belk explained. "He was my mother's grandfather, and he was a captain in the American Army under Colonel Davie. Right at this place—" he turned

SARAH WALKUP BELK

ABEL NELSON WASHINGTON
BELK

DR. JOHN M. BELK IN 1895

WILLIAM HENRY BELK IN 1895

to point off toward the right, "down the hill there a little piece, where Captain Wauchope's mill stood, they had a skirmish with the British soldiers under Tarleton, and the Americans killed a large number of them that day. That was in September, 1780, just a few days before the British reached Charlotte, where they ran into a pack of trouble and pretty soon had to get out and head back fast into South Carolina."

A marker in the field near the present house records the skirmish. It was one of the more dramatic fights of the Revolution in the South, and it brought into brief but furious collision two of the most spirited cavalrymen of that war, Britain's "Bloody" Banastre Tarleton and the Waxhaw country's own young and lively and later to be distinguished William Richardson Davie.

Tarleton, furious at the opposition the advancing Redcoats had encountered in the Carolina back country, had seized Captain Wauchope's plantation while the captain was away with Davie's horsemen. Mrs. Wauchope, the sister of General Andrew Pickens, who had been contributing heavily to the cause of making the lives of the British invaders of the Carolinas both miserable and precarious, was a prisoner with her children in their own home.

And then, quite unexpectedly and while the British were at ease and many of their weapons were stacked about the farmyard, Captain Wauchope came home, bringing hard-riding guests with him. The clash was sharp. In a few minutes Davie's men had killed sixty Redcoats and captured many excellent horses and a large stand of arms. But a strong British force in the vicinity, having learned quickly of the fighting at Wauchope's, was riding to the rescue of Tarleton's troops, and Davie's riders had to leave hurriedly.

During the fighting around the mill and the farmhouse, according to surviving stories of the skirmish, the Wauchope home caught fire. Margaret Pickens Wauchope and her children had to rush outside, where they had a short and hurried reunion with the captain before he had to dash away with Colonel Davie.

Various histories refer to this skirmish at Captain Wauchope's. Some speak of the "Wahab" fight, some spell the name "Wahub," and others call it "Walkup." Marquis James in his *Andrew Jackson: The Border Captain* gives the name correctly: Wauchope.

"I don't know just when the name was changed," Mr. Belk said that afternoon as he walked about the yard of the old Wauchope place and talked of his mother's people. "I'm sorry they changed it. Of course, what they were doing was simplifying it; that's what they were figuring on when they made it Walkup. But I wish they had let it stay Wauchope. It's a good name. The Wauchopes were fine people back in Scotland and still are, I understand."

In the early days when old John Belk joined the tide of immigration spreading westward from Charleston and the Low Country that merged with the stream surging southward from Pennsylvania to establish homes in this Carolina back country, the region was known as "The Garden of the Waxhaws."

The Waxhaw territory lay between the Rocky River and the Catawba, and before the coming of the white settlers was inhabited by the Waxhaw Indians. In about 1740 the Waxhaws were almost wiped out by an epidemic of smallpox, a disease previously unknown to the tribe, and the few remaining families joined the Catawba Indians and other neighboring tribes. When this section was abandoned, the land agents, finding such a fertile region unmolested by savages and claimed by no one, began to advertise to bring desirable settlers to the district. The Scotch-Irish settlers in Pennsylvania were having difficulty with the French-dominated Indians and found that the peace-loving Quakers were of little assistance so they migrated to what was called "The Waxhaw Settlement," now a portion of Union County, North Carolina, and Lancaster County, South Carolina. At the time of the arrival of the white settlers in 1751, this territory was covered with a massive forest of oak, pine, and other timber. There was no underbrush and the trees were large and so widely spaced that a view from the ground of this gently sweeping region was usually unbroken except by the large tree trunks. For grazing the section was unsurpassed as the grass grew almost waist high and the country was covered with a thick growth of wild pea vines. Here the pioneer hunter found game in abundance and fish in every stream. Later the land proved rich in minerals also and the Waxhaws became widely known for its gold mines.

"It's a good section—good country," Mr. Belk will say in describing his native community. "The folks down in the Waxhaws are good people, hard-working, God-fearing folks. They're solid. They believe in doing what's right. Of course, in any community there's always a fellow here and there that don't do right and don't want to do right, but these Waxhaw folks are generally first-rate people—not high-flyers, but just good solid folks."

4

ACROSS THE LONG YEARS AND WITH WARM AFFECTION
Henry Belk remembers the one-room schoolhouse and his
first teacher.

"She was Miss Mollie Patterson, the daughter of old
Preacher Patterson," he recalls. "She was one of the ladies
in the community, and she was a good teacher. That's the
way it was back in those times; the teachers were just men
and women who lived about in the community. And they were
generally mighty good teachers, too. They made us learn, and
they made us behave."

"After Miss Mollie I had a man for a teacher, a Mr. Finley. I remember we studied reading and ciphering and the Blue Back Speller. And that old Blue Back Speller was hard to beat. We had what they called phonetic spelling. We spelled by the sound of a word. They tell me they don't teach spelling that way now; they say the children nowadays learn a word just by the way it looks, just like they learn a man's face. And it's my opinion a lot of them nowadays can't spell. I think it's a pity they don't go back to the old phonetic system. A lot of good spellers learned that way."

The first schools Mr. Belk attended were typical of the Carolinas and the country in general at that period.

"Scholars of all ages went to the same school and usually had the same teacher," Mr. Belk recalls. "There were the beginners, little boys and girls whose legs were too short to reach the floor when they sat on the split log benches, and there were grown men and women, leastways they looked grown to us little ones in the room.

"And there were all kinds of books, too, and each scholar did his studying out loud. The schoolhouse sounded like a swarm of bees—and bumble-bees, at that. Some were reading and some were ciphering, and you never heard such a droning as those scholars of all ages made in the little schoolhouse. But we learned a lot in those 'old field' schools, as they were called then. And in some respects, I wouldn't be surprised if they beat our schools of today."

Much of the instruction in the fundamentals the Belk boys received from their mother, Mr. Belk remembers with an affection strengthened by the years.

"My mother was a great woman," he declares. "She was a young woman when my father died, and she had a heavy responsibility. Soon after the war was over we lost most of our property. But my mother wouldn't give up. She went to see one of my uncles and got him to bid the farm in when it was put up for sale. Afterwards we bought it back, but it was a long time after we started the store before Brother John and I got all that debt paid off."

Under her agreement with her former slaves, Mrs. Belk employed a white man to direct the farming operations. In accordance with her plans, she engaged John R. Simpson to manage the farm, and in 1866 Sarah Walkup Belk, now thirty, married Mr. Simpson.

In the years that followed, Sarah Belk Simpson again tasted the bitterness and agony of bereavement. Her twins died at birth, and she lost two other children, Robert and Kitty, in early childhood. Elizabeth (Mrs. George B. McClellan, of Monroe, who died in 1949) and Will Simpson (who died in 1950) were the only children of this marriage who survived to reach adulthood.

Life in the days that followed the ending of the war was not altogether grim, for it had its joys and its satisfactions, but for the five children it meant regular tasks to be done and much work with their play. The Simpson children, like the three Belk boys, were to get their first training in books, as in living, from their mother. She had been educated at the Carolina Female College in Ansonville, North Carolina, shortly after that institution had opened its doors in 1851.

"Mother taught us a lot at home when we were small," Mr. Belk recalls. "She used to teach the Negroes, too. She wanted everybody around her to know how to read and write. She especially wanted the Negroes to know how to read the Bible. I well remember how she used to put in almost all the spare time we could get teaching us, telling us stories, Bible stories and other stories, and helping us with our lessons. It was mighty hard times we came up in, but Mother didn't get discouraged. She never would give up. And she was determined for us to get an education."

In 1873, when Henry Belk was eleven years old, the family left the farm in Lancaster County, South Carolina, and moved to Monroe in Union Counnty, North Carolina. Tom Belk was thirteen and John, who had been a baby in the cradle when his father died, was nine. At this time conditions in the South were little improved. Politically and economically, the section was staggering under the heavy burden of the lost war. Alien, vindictive, and evil forces were striving completely to destroy its culture. It was a cruel and tragic period, particularly so for a child whose mind was still in a highly impressionable state. It produced injuries and left wounds that decades would never entirely heal.

"We had it mighty tough," Henry Belk says of those long days of his youth. "And Sherman's gang had killed my father. I couldn't forget that. And after the war was over the Carpetbaggers and other ruffians from the North kept preying on us and plaguing us. I've never been able to forget—or completely to forgive either, I'm afraid—the wrongs done in those terrible days to us prostrate folks in the South. It wasn't the best people in the North who were responsible for the treatment we got; most of them probably knew little about what was going on down here. But in that period, more than during the war years even, many southerners grew to hate all Yankees, and it's hard for us who were children then to forget even after three-quarters of a century. It's mighty hard for us to overcome our prejudices. That just goes to show what a strong impression the sort of things that happened to us in the South right after the Civil War leave on the mind of a child. It has a lot to do with what type of a man that child is going to grow up to be. It makes you wonder what kind of men and women the children in Europe today will be twenty and thirty and forty years from now."

At Monroe young Belk continued his schooling.

"Miss Maggie Harrison was my teacher at first," he remembers. "Then I had Miss Sanders, who taught in another room. Later I had old Squire McAuley. He was strict, and he made his scholars study and learn. There wasn't much foolishness about going to school in those days. The scholars had to behave, and they had to study. Spelling was one of the main studies. Ciphering was another; I don't think they call it that any more. But that's what we called learning how to figure. And, as I said, they certainly believed in spelling then, and took great pride in being good spellers; and we had a lot of fine spellers too.

"I remember at Monroe spelling was the last thing in the afternoon before school let out. That's when they'd have a spelling bee. They would divide the scholars, the big ones, that is, into two lines facing each other. Sometimes the teacher would choose the spellers and sometimes each side would have a captain and they'd take time about choosing the best spellers.

"The teacher would stand up between the two lines of scholars and give out the words. When a fellow missed a word, he'd have to sit down. The last man up was the champion and his side won. We had hard words, too. And we had a certain way to follow in spelling the words given out to us. We had to pronounce the word first; that was to show that you knew what the word was that you were going to try to spell. Then we had to spell the first syllable and pronounce it, and so on, syllable by syllable, until we had spelled the word. Like this: the teacher would give out the word *baker*. Then we'd say: 'Baker. b-a, ba; k-e-r, ker; baker.' I wish they'd get back to that way of teaching spelling. I believe we'd have better spellers, and judging by a lot of the college boys and girls of today, we certainly need better spellers. Many of them certainly can't spell."

Later Mrs. Simpson sent Henry to live with her brother, Dr. Henry Clay Walkup, in the near-by Sharon section of adjacent Mecklenburg County, so that he might have the advantage of the excellent school that was being conducted in that community.

"My mother believed in education," says Mr. Belk, recalling those days. "They were hard times back there, and there were few opportunities for schooling. My uncle, Dr. Henry Clay Walkup—my mother's folks were Whigs and they named my uncle Henry Clay—was practicing medicine up in the Sharon community in Mecklenburg County and he suggested to my mother that she let me stay with him and go to school up there. They had a good school. It had a mighty fine reputation all around the country. And so my mother sent me up to Sharon to live with my uncle and attend school there."

He still recalls his first teacher at Sharon.

"He was Professor Hugh K. Reid. His son Banks is living in Charlotte and I see him every now and then. Professor Reid was a good teacher. He believed in keeping order, and everybody respected him. I liked him. But I still remember that he did me wrong one day. He made a mistake. And I almost jumped on him and had a fight. But I didn't. I guess I was just a little afraid to tackle him.

"One day some fellow in the room did something that made a boy laugh out loud. Professor Reid thought I was the one that had done it. So he came over to me and pulled my ear. It made me mad at the time. I told him he had the wrong man, that I wasn't the one who had made the boy laugh. And I guess I looked like I was about ready to jump on him. He didn't say anything; he just looked at me a second and walked away. It's a wonder that I didn't up and start fighting him. I was pretty hot-tempered in those days and it made me right mad when he pulled my ear. And I thought too that he ought to have admitted his mistake. And I reckon I still do. But Professor Reid was a good teacher and a good man, and he helped me a lot.

"Mr. Joe Rankin, my next teacher at Sharon, was a good one, too. The teachers back in those days, in fact, generally commanded the respect of the scholars and the community. They were the big men in the community and everybody looked up to the professor at the school."

From Sharon young Belk returned to Monroe for further schooling.

"The school at Monroe in those days would correspond to our present high schools," he points out. "I went to school there and got ready to go off to college, and my mother was mighty anxious for me to go. But by the time I was ready for college, a lot of things had happened to me, and I knew what I wanted to do."

In August of 1875 young Tom Belk, Henry's older brother, died shortly before his fifteenth birthday and Sarah Belk again felt the agony of personal loss. In September of the same year, Thomas Milburn Belk, grandfather of the Belk children, also died. He was buried in the graveyard of old Shiloh among his loved ones and on his tombstone was carved: "Mark the perfect man and behold the upright, for the end of man is peace." Although Old Tom had been a wealthy man before the war, the Reconstruction years had found him stripped of most of his possessions with the exception of some land. However, he left a hundred dollars to each of the Belk boys to be paid on their twenty-first birthdays. Henry does not recall that he ever received his portion of his grandfather's estate. The hundred dollars might have been the deciding factor in sending him to college—he did not go because of lack of money for board and books—or it would have added materially to the money which he was saving to buy merchandise for the store which he hoped to open someday.

II

COUNTRY MERCHANT

5

Henry Belk likes to say that he knew from early childhood what he wanted to do when he grew up. "I don't remember when I didn't want to be a merchant. It just always seemed to appeal to me. I'm sure that as a child I never thought of doing anything else when I got grown."

That is the way he puts it now, but it may well be that the kind of life he led as a boy during the Reconstruction years had much to do with his wanting to become a merchant. In a time of such desperate poverty, bartering and swapping were the way to keep alive, and a keen youngster like Henry

Belk would not have been slow in learning—and enjoying—how to make a good trade. And with so little of the world's goods to be had, even the small stock of a store in Monroe, with its less than a thousand inhabitants, must have seemed like riches indeed. It is no wonder that the small boy's love of "playing store" became in Henry Belk a life's ambition.

By the time he was fourteen, in 1876, young Henry must have felt that he had grown to man's estate. Light brown-haired and blue-eyed, he was shooting out of his boy's clothes on the way to the lean six-footer of his young manhood. Though his mother had remarried and her husband was head of the house in which he lived, the deaths of his grandfather and his older brother in 1875 left Henry the oldest male Belk in the immediate family, and it was time for him to do something about it. Sarah Simpson was insistent that her son get a proper education, capped off by a college degree, but Henry saw no reason why he could not get a job at once and carry on his studies on the side.

For the South, 1876 was a crucial year. In the presidential elections that fall, the Democratic candidate, Samuel Tilden, received more popular votes than his Republican rival, but lost the election—many contended he was counted out—in the electoral vote. With tempers running high over the disputed election, the new president, Rutherford B. Hayes, agreed to take away the last of the Federal troops that were "protecting" the Reconstruction government, and early the next year Reconstruction was officially ended. Though Henry Belk was never keenly interested in politics, he must have heard much of the hot political arguments of that time. Having been brought up on a farm and living in a farming center, he would have known that this was a bad time for the farmers. The high cotton prices that immediately followed the Civil War had broken, and cotton prices were in a decline that was to last twenty years. Being a boy, Henry would have devoured all the talk of railroads and railroad building that he heard about him. Monroe itself was on the new railroad—just completed two years before—from Wilmington to Charlotte; and all over North Carolina and the rest of the South, the old railroads that had fallen to pieces in the war were being restored, and new ones were being built and projected. Much of the talk that Henry heard would have been about the town of Charlotte, twenty-five miles northwest of Monroe, and all the railroad lines that were centering there. The population of Charlotte was about five thousand, which made it the biggest town in all of western North Carolina.

In 1876 Henry Belk probably had not heard—and if he had, he would not have attached any great significance to it —that three years before a young man named Washington Duke had set up a tobacco factory in Durham, and that just the year before another young man named R. J. Reynolds had set up another in the town of Winston, which had recently got its first outside railroad connection. He was probably unaware that over the Piedmont of North Carolina and South Carolina a scattering of cotton mills was springing up, some of them rebuilt from before the war, others new. Monroe itself was chiefly the county seat and trading center for the farmers of Union County, North Carolina, who were raising cotton for the market and corn and wheat and some cattle for their own use.

As Mr. Belk recalls it, there was no special difficulty in getting his first job.

"I started to work for Mr. B. D. Heath at Monroe. He was a good merchant and he had the leading store down in that part of the country. I had been wanting to get into the store business so I could trade and traffic, which I figured I was cut out to do. So I went to see Mr. Heath and told him I wanted to learn the business."

It was considered a good job and five dollars a month was

excellent pay for a fourteen-year-old boy in 1876, especially for one who had had no experience in store work and was just starting out to learn the dry goods business. But it demanded hard work and long hours, for store hours were governed by no state or federal or merchants' association's laws or rules.

"The stores opened early in the morning to catch the first folks stirring about and they stayed open as long as anybody was still stirring," Mr. Belk recalls. "There wasn't much time left a fellow except to eat and sleep. About all the rest of the time a fellow spent at the store. This new business of forty hours a week and over-time pay had never been heard of until long after I was a boy working for Mr. Heath. The time we worked at the store was more than double forty hours."

Young Belk worked three months at five dollars a month. At the end of that first quarter—and he delights to this day in telling the story—he had saved $14.85. If he remembers when he made his first million, he never speaks of it, but he recalls with warmest satisfaction those three five-dollar monthly payments he received from the Monroe merchant and particularly the fact that he saved all but fifteen cents.

"I guess I'd have saved the entire fifteen dollars if it hadn't been that I wanted to buy something to eat," he hastens to add in describing those first wages. "I don't remember just now what it was that I spent the fifteen cents for; I guess it must have been for an apple now and then."

He must have been a good worker and an enthusiastic apprentice, for Mr. Heath raised him the next quarter. It was a tremendous raise, too, from fifteen to twenty-five dollars a quarter.

"I felt so good about it and so confident that I was going to become a merchant that I got extravagant during those three months, for out of that twenty-five dollars I spent

SARAH WALKUP BELK SIMPSON in her eighty-fifth year

Family group, 1927. Standing: R. J. BELK (in rear), Miss JOHN BELK, PINKEY BOWDEN (in rear), SARAH HOUSTON, unidentified woman, Mrs. W. D. SIMPSON (in rear), Mrs. NEALIE BELK STEVENS, Dr. W. D. SIMPSON, Dr. JOHN M. BELK, W. H. BELK, Mrs. W. H. BELK, Miss HENRY BELK, MOLLIE HOUSTON (in foreground). Seated: SARAH STEVENS, Mrs. SARAH WALKUP BELK SIMPSON, SARAH BELK, unidentified child, IRWIN BELK, JOHN STEVENS exactly one-fourth, six dollars and twenty-five cents. But maybe I wasn't extravagant as that sounds, because if I remember rightly I bought a suit of clothes with that money."

Before many more months had passed the young merchant had made another sharp advance in the world of selling. He had continued to do so well that Mr. Heath had given him a 50 per cent raise. Now he was getting twelve dollars and a half each month.

"That was pretty good money, too," he maintains. "I was still just a boy, but by now I was all the more certain that when I grew up and got in business for myself I was going to be a merchant.

"But all this time I had been studying, too, every chance I had, and getting ready to go off to school, and it was about this time, as I remember, that the county commissioners of Union County selected me as the representative of the county to go to the University at Chapel Hill on a scholarship."

He went one day to Mr. Heath and told him that he was thinking of entering the University. He explained that he was still planning to be a merchant but that the thought he should go off to college and finish his schooling. Then he would come back to Monroe and continue his interrupted career as a merchant.

But Mr. Heath argued against it.

"Henry," he said solemnly, "you are getting along fine. You are learning the store business fast, and I'm afraid it would be a mistake for you to drop it now and go off to school. You'll like as not get to studying at Chapel Hill and the first thing you know you'll be getting interested in doing some other kind of work, and it appears to me, Henry, that you're cut out to run a store some time. I believe you'd be making a bad mistake to quit now while you're getting along so well."

He offered young Belk another raise. This time it was a 33⅓ per cent boost in his wages. He had been getting thirty-seven dollars and a half a quarter. The Monroe storekeeper offered him fifty dollars.

Henry Belk considered the situation carefully. Conditions were not promising—they were just barely making out at home. And there were the younger children who would have to be educated too. His brother John, in particular, was turning out to be a good student, who should not be denied all the education he needed. Henry felt keenly his responsibility as the oldest child. And when he talked with his mother about going to the University, she revealed that she planned to sell some of the Belk land to pay his expenses at Chapel Hill. The scholarship he had won paid only the tuition; it provided nothing for board and clothing.

He decided to remain with Mr. Heath.

One day when Mr. Belk was telling this story, someone in the group listening suggested that if he had gone off to school he would probably have settled down later to a job as school teacher or bookkeeper or in some other career usually demanding small compensation.

"Well, I wouldn't say that," he countered. "I might have done better. I was determined to be a storekeeper. I would probably have come back after I finished my schooling at Chapel Hill and gone into the store business. And, as I say, I might have done better after having gone to the University. I believe mighty strongly in education. That's why I was especially anxious for my children to get as good educations as they would take. Next to being good Christians, I think there's nothing better for young people than for them to get good educations."

It was while Henry Belk was still in his teens working for Mr. Heath that he made his first independent venture.

"It didn't amount to much," he always hastens to point out. "Mr. Heath had a brother-in-law named Hugh Wilson, like myself, just a boy. We decided to start us up a store. We bought some fruit and candy and rented a little stand and started in business. There was a fellow in Monroe by the name of Will Houston that we hired to run our store for us. As I say, we were both boys and we didn't know much about running a business; but I soon came to the conclusion that we weren't going to do any good with our store. I didn't think Houston knew much about running it. So I sold out my part to Wilson and he didn't make any success of it and soon liquidated it. That was my first store, if you call that a store. It certainly wasn't much of one, any way you look at it."

Henry Belk's apprenticeship with Mr. Heath lasted nearly twelve years. His was not a spectacular advance, but Monroe was not a spectacular place, and when, by the time he was twenty-five, he had become Mr. Heath's buyer and right-hand man at a salary of forty dollars a month, he had attained a position of respect in the community. More important to him, with his stubborn ambition to be a merchant, he had learned the elements of his business—the value of merchandise, what people wanted, how to deal with them. Of course the needs that brought buyers to Mr. Heath's store were fairly simple, even for that time. The women wanted chiefly yard goods—calicos, ginghams, muslins—along with ribbons, lace, and "notions." Women's clothes were made at home, by the purchaser if she were poor or by a sewing woman if she could afford one. A farmer or mechanic needed work clothes from time to time, but one store-bought suit for Sundays and holidays would last for years. Then there were shoes for both sexes, kitchen and table ware, household equipment, and some of the simpler luxuries. But even though the line was not elaborate, it was necessary to please the customer as to quality and price and service.

And while Mr. Heath did the important travelling for the store, Henry Belk had also managed to get around. He had been learning how certain merchants in other parts of the country—like John Wanamaker in Philadelphia for whom he would have great admiration all his life—were bringing new ideas into merchandising. He could see how bad, both for customer and merchant, was the "time" system of selling goods to farmers, a system that prevailed in Monroe, as it did in most of the South. The farmer sought credit, asked the merchant to "carry" him through the winter and spring months and gave him as security a mortgage upon his fall crops, perhaps his livestock and farm equipment. The merchant in turn felt that he had to charge higher prices for the goods provided the farmer on this "time" basis. The farmer, unable to pay cash, grumbled at what he considered the unfairness of the system, but paid the prices demanded—if he could. When the crops were poor or the price of cotton was low he might be unable to "pay out." Then the merchant took his mules or his cow or perhaps his farm tools in satisfaction of the mortgage. And the farmer had nothing with which to start a new crop. It was a vicious system. Young Henry Belk, observing it and its effects, wondered if some other system could not be devised that would be more profitable to the merchant and to the farmer, more profitable to the one in fact because it was more profitable to the other. While he measured out calico or fitted coarse work shoes to calloused feet, Henry Belk sought to devise better ways of conducting a store business.

With his head full of ideas that needed testing, he knew it was time to be making a start. But it was a difficult decision for young Belk.

"I thought about it a good while. I was making pretty good money for a young man in those days and I was certain I had Mr. Heath's confidence, for I was ahead of everybody in the store except him. I realized I'd be cutting loose from a good job. But I was determined to get into business for myself. I figured I might put in some new licks around Monroe. So

I made up my mind that I would quit and start up my own store."

He went to Mr. Heath one day and told him what he had decided. He reminded the Monroe storekeeper that when he had started working for him he had told him he wanted to learn the merchandising business. He was not leaving because of dissatisfaction but because he felt that it was time he was striking out on his own.

That was early in May, 1888. He was well along in his twelfth year with the Monroe merchant.

"I had traded with Mr. Heath on the basis of the year's running from September to September. I told him I would stay out the year if he wanted me to but that I'd like to quit then if possible and get started for myself.

" 'I'd like for you to stay on with me, Henry,' he told me, 'but I won't hold you until the end of the year; you needn't stay until September if you don't want to, and if you think best and want to do it that way you can quit any time now you want to.' "

Young Belk told him he was planning to quit as soon as possible, and then he asked him if he'd lend him five hundred dollars. He had saved seven hundred and fifty, he told his employer, but that would hardly be enough capital with which to begin his new business venture.

The merchant was evasive. He told Henry Belk that he was planning to leave on a business trip the next morning, and he promised that during the night he would consider the request carefully and let him know before he left whether or not he would lend him the money.

When Mr. Heath the next morning failed to mention the request for a loan, young Belk approached him again and asked what he had decided to do about it.

"Henry," his employer replied, "I'd let you have that money as quick as I would my brother. I trust you. I know you'd pay me back. But, Henry, if I let you have the money, I'd be giving you a stick to hit me over the head with. I just can't afford to do that. Henry, I can't let you have the money."

"So I went to see Colonel John McCain's widow," Mr. Belk continues the story, "and I asked her to lend me that five hundred dollars I needed. She agreed to let me have it and I agreed to pay her 10 per cent interest. That was in the days before they had laws concerning interest. You just paid whatever you had to pay in order to get the money when you needed it.

"I rented a store building twenty-two feet by seventy, got it cleaned up pretty well and fixed it up for opening, and then I started getting my stock together for the store. I had that seven hundred and fifty dollars I had saved during the years I had been working for Mr. Heath and I had the five hundred I had borrowed from Widow McCain. But I figured I needed more money for getting a stock to start off with. About that time I learned that Captain John Austin had a considerable stock of merchandise left over from his store. He had been in business with two others, but the business hadn't done well and so they had discontinued it and divided up what was left. Captain Austin had about three thousand dollars worth of stock.

"I went to see Captain Austin and made a trade with him for that stock. With the money I had saved and borrowed and Captain Austin's stock I was ready to get set up in the store business.

"I opened for business on May 29, 1888. I called my store the New York Racket. You see, back in those days they called stores like mine racket stores. The word racket back then didn't have the meaning it has nowadays. The reason I named it the New York Racket, I reckon, was because New York was a big city and I figured that by calling it the New York

Racket everybody would think that sounded big. I figured it would help my trade."

The name may have helped, but it was probably hard work and application of his time, brains, and brawn that helped most. At any rate, it was soon apparent that young Henry Belk, starting out for himself in his own store at twenty-six, would shortly be a factor in the business life of his community.

Before Christmas of that same year, little more than six months after he had established his store, Henry Belk sat down one night after closing time and figured how he stood.

"I found out I had done all right, too," he likes to recall. "I had paid off Captain Austin his three thousand, the Widow McCain her five hundred, and I had thirty-three hundred on top of that. That wasn't so bad for a young fellow starting out with seven hundred and fifty, was it? The way I figure it, I had made better than 400 per cent. I'll tell you what—" Mr. Belk will pause and grin broadly as he says it—"I never have done that well since."

6

W HEN TWENTY-SIX-YEAR-OLD HENRY BELK SET UP FOR himself he had, in addition to his capital of seven hundred and fifty dollars, intangible assets of great value and some merchandising ideas that were considered highly dubious by his friends. Chief among the assets were his absolute honesty and integrity—qualities that were instilled in him by the stout Presbyterian faith that he learned from his mother. Another was his reputation as a hard and willing worker. In a community that took its religion seriously and knew, from the hard life of Reconstruction and after, that those who did not work could not eat, such a reputation counted for much. To this day Mr. Belk insists that these qualities are all a man needs for success. That they are the ingredients for a happy and useful life cannot be denied, but it is likely that it was his radical ideas of merchandising that kept him from ending his career as a highly respected merchant in Monroe and led him eventually to the leadership of a system of more than three hundred stores throughout the South.

He knew the people that he was dealing with and what kind of merchandise they wanted. Monroe had grown in his twelve years with Mr. Heath—it was now between two and three thousand in size—and Union County along with it. But though it was on the edge of the Piedmont belt in which cotton mills had been springing up all through the eighties, it was still what it had been when he started to work, a trading center for farmers whose life was tied up in cotton and corn, with a little wheat. It was not plantation country—that was farther south—but a county of small farmers who were still mostly of Scotch-Irish and English descent, like his own people. And they had not been prosperous—cotton had not sold much over ten cents a pound for the past ten years. They would be looking for the necessities rather than the luxuries, and they would want the best quality at the most reasonable price.

That he could give them—he knew this from his experience with Mr. Heath. But he proposed two innovations. First he would mark his merchandise clearly with its retail price—no haggling at the counter—and there would be no question about taking back anything that did not satisfy the customer. If a man bought a work shirt, took it home, found that it was not what he thought it would be or for any other reason did not want to keep it, then let him bring it back. Take back the shirt and give the man his money. And do it pleasantly. Make the customer feel that you were really anxious to please him. Then he would not hesitate to continue trading with you.

That was enough of a new thing in itself, but his other merchandising idea was far more radical. He was going to sell for cash only. He would have no "time" business; he would not "carry" anybody. He would have no accounts to record, no notes to accept, no mortgages on farm crops and farm animals to foreclose, no customers distressed because he had taken their hard-earned property, no one angry and threatening because he had dispossessed them.

"It was a new thing in our part of the country," Mr. Belk points out. "I don't think anybody had ever tried it out down this way and mighty few anywhere. My friends came to me and told me that it wouldn't work.

" 'Henry,' they said, 'you'll go broke. Folks aren't accustomed to that way of trading. They won't like it and they won't trade with you. They won't have the money to trade with, in fact. It'll put you out of business before you get started!'

"That's what they said. But I was determined to try it out. I figured it would work. It would save me money and it would save the customers money, I told my friends. There was a man in Philadelphia that I had been watching. I figured he was a mighty good merchant. He had started up his store about the time I was born—a year before, I believe. He had started in business with a man named Brown, his brother-in-law, as I remember. They had built up a fine trade. I had been watching him and that was the way he was operating his business. He didn't appear to be on the way to going broke, either. His name was Wanamaker—John Wanamaker. And he was a great man, in more ways than one. I've always had a great respect for him."

But it was one thing for Mr. Wanamaker in Philadelphia or other merchants in northern cities to try the cash idea. There were factories there with payrolls, and a growing army of white-collar workers getting paid by the week, so that a merchant could count on a steady flow of customers with cash. It was altogether different, and a daring gamble, to count on the same plan's working in a small community of farmers feeling the pressure of low farm prices. But Henry Belk was as stubborn as his friends were critical, and when he counted up his earnings at the end of 1888, he could feel that he had proved his point.

The business continued to grow—not spectacularly, but steadily. And Henry Belk worked. Through the long hours when the store was open—from daylight until well into the night—and then later into the night after it had been closed for the day.

He demanded more of himself than he demanded of any of those who worked for him. There was no work about the store that he did not do. He sold goods, wrapped packages, saw to the unpacking of goods received from the north, helped place them on the counters, priced them and did the countless small and large things that must be done about a store. And he did the buying, of course. He visited the markets, mainly in Baltimore and New York and some times Philadelphia, and he calculated with shrewd eye and practiced fingers the quality and price of innumerable yards of material, suits, shirts, dresses, ribbons, and velvets.

He was the proprietor of the store, the man upon whom all responsibility of operating the business rested, and he was likewise clerk, bookkeeper, buyer, and often sweeper. Soon the task had become too heavy for one man to handle, even a young and strong and enthusiastic one. He hired help—some half a dozen employees, he recalls, before many months—but what he needed was someone he could trust with a share of the responsibility.

About this time he happened to take a trip. Henry Belk is convinced that it was the most profitable trip he ever made, that visit almost sixty years ago to his brother John. To this day he delights in telling about it.

"Brother John had finished his course in medicine at New York University and had settled down to practice at a little place in Anson County called Morven," he points out. "I had been helping him with his expenses while he was in school and I was still working for Mr. Heath, and he had been paying me back ever since he had started practicing. Finally he had paid me up to the last penny.

"Well, I decided to go down and visit him. I remember the night I got there it was cold and rainy—a mighty bad night. And late that night Brother John got a call to come out to see a sick man who lived several miles back in the country. It was such a bad night that I suggested to Brother John that he ought to send the man something to ease his pain and then go out to see him the next morning.

"'No, Brother Henry,' he said to me, 'I'll have to go out to see him tonight. I am a doctor and I took a doctor's oath to help the sick regardless of how it might inconvenience me or whether or not I ever got paid for my services. I've got to go see the man tonight and help him if I can.'

"And Brother John went. When he got back late in the night, cold and wet, I said to him, 'Brother John, I can tell you a better way of making a living than being a doctor. You go in with me in the store business.'

"We talked the matter over pro and con and I argued with him that it would be better for him to get into the store business, that he had better prospects as a merchant than as a doctor, and after a while he agreed to go in with me. That was the best trip I ever made. It was a good thing for both of us, I am sure, our going into business together. I know it was a good thing for me and I think Brother John never regretted taking the step.

"So that was how Belk Brothers was started. Brother John

went in with me in 1891, with one-half interest in the business, and we stayed together until his death. We always got along mighty well together. I never knew a finer man than Brother John."

Whether medicine lost a great practitioner in John M. Belk no one will ever know, but the partnership of the brothers was unique in its complete trust, its sharing of talents, and its eventual huge success. Their relationship was too close for it to be said that one specialized in one side of the business and the other in another. They formed an ideal partnership because their temperaments balanced one another.

"I was pretty quick-tempered and I had a tendency to make snap-judgment decisions," Henry Belk recalls. "But Brother John was cool and easy-tempered, and he always took time to think things out. Once he reached a decision, you could depend upon its being the right one. He was a good influence on me."

In matters of any considerable importance the brothers would never take independent action. They invariably, as Mr. Belk terms it now, "talked things over." And they never had any real difficulty in agreeing upon the proper course to take once they had discussed the problem in detail.

Dr. John Belk's return to Monroe enlivened the Belk clan, for he brought with him his bride of two years and their one-year-old daughter, Nealie Belk, the first of seven daughters born of his marriage. Henry Belk continued unmarried —he confesses that he was too wrapped up in his business to think of marriage at that time—and lived with his mother.

As the brothers' business continued to prosper under the impetus of Henry's new ideas, and as the brothers themselves became popular and respected citizens of the community in which she had reared them, Sarah Simpson could take pride

in the fruits of her faith and sacrifice in the war and Reconstruction.

In their small store in Monroe, in the early nineties, the
Belk brothers worked out the pattern of operations that was
to characterize the entire Belk system. The underlying philosophy was Henry Belk's, and he has summarized it in his
own homely way:

"Our idea was to sell goods just as cheap as we could and
at the same time make a small profit, and to have a quick
turnover. We figured that if we could undersell the other
fellow and get cash for our goods, we'd be doing better than
to accept credit business and run the risk of losing out in the
fall, when the farmers sold their crops, in the hope of making
a bigger profit. It worked out fine, too. Our customers liked
it better. When a fellow buys something and pays cash, he
just naturally feels good. He doesn't have that trade hanging
over him. He's through. And if on top of that he knows he
can bring the goods back if they aren't what he wanted, and
get his money back, he feels pretty satisfied about his trade.
That was our idea and we found that it worked."

But a good idea is one thing—putting it into practice is
another. The Belks had to work out for themselves a way to
handle a cash business, quickly enough to please the customer
and accurately enough to make sure that the right charge was
made and paid. Perhaps the best picture of how this store
operated on the floor—and also how the Belks trained their
employees—can be obtained from a story told by Torrence E.
Hemby, a Monroe youngster who started with the Belks
and is now president of the American Trust Company of
Charlotte.

"I think I was thirteen, and I was wrapper boy," Mr.
Hemby says. "The wrapping counter was right down in front
of and under the platform where the cashier sat. The order
of importance in the store was this: check-boy, wrapper boy,

cashier, and clerk. It was my job to take a package from the check-boy, who had brought it from the clerk who made the sale, look at the ticket and see that the price charged the customer corresponded with the price marked on the article, and if it did, wrap up the article and give it back to the check-boy, who carried it back to the customer.

"I'll never forget how embarrassed I was one day. The wrapping counter was right close to Dr. John Belk's office; in fact, they had stacked bolts of cloth high at the ends of the counter and along in front of Dr. Belk's office to help make it more private. Well, this day I had just wrapped a hat that one of the check-boys had brought. Dr. Belk was standing over near the end of the counter, a little behind the bolts of cloth, and I hadn't seen him. He stepped out from the corner just as I was finishing with the hat.

" 'Young man,' he said to me, 'what's the price of that hat?'

"I was terribly embarrassed. I hadn't checked the price marked on the band inside the hat. It was pretty soon after I had started to work and I don't remember whether at that time I had been instructed to check the prices or not, but anyway, I was certainly embarrassed when I didn't know the price of the hat.

"Then Dr. Belk told me that it was my duty to check the prices of all articles I wrapped against the prices shown on the sales tickets to see that they agreed. He told me I had an important job in the store. He was kind and gentle but he was also firm and he impressed me even then as being a man of fine business habits and a very orderly and excellent mind."

But even more important than the system is the spirit with which an organization is run, and here the most revealing story concerns another Union County boy who had his first job with the Belks and later became one of the South's leading jurists. Henry Belk himself likes to tell this anecdote about the boyhood of Judge John J. Parker:

"John was always a polite and considerate boy. That's the way a boy learning the store business—or any other boy, for that matter—ought to be. It's good to be that way, and it's mighty good business, too.

"Well, one day it was bad and rainy and one of John's duties was to take an umbrella over to the edge of the sidewalk and help the ladies get out of their buggies without getting wet. John would help them out and hold the umbrella over them until they got inside the store.

"This day John had been doing that. When an old colored woman came along and stopped in front of the store, John went out and helped her out of the buggy and held the umbrella over her until she got out of the rain. It was a nice thing to do, and it was just like John to do a thing like that.

"But one of the clerks made some remark about it—not bad, but in a sort of teasing way. Brother John happened to hear him. In fact, Brother John seemed to have an uncanny way of hearing things around the store. And he didn't like it. He knew that John wanted to be a lawyer when he grew up.

" 'Don't let him tease you, John,' Brother John said to him. 'When he's still clerking you'll be on the Supreme Court, son, and I mean the Supreme Court of the United States.'

"Well, John Parker was nominated for a place on the Supreme Court by President Hoover, and it was just tough luck because of the narrowness of some of those senators that he isn't on it today. He has more sense than many a one that's been on it."

Although the Belks certainly did not realize it at this time, the Monroe store was the recruiting station and training school for many of the top executives of the future Belk organizations. It was a perfectly natural development. Henry Belk himself was a farm boy whose thoughts had turned to

First Belk Store, Monroe, North Carolina, 1897. Frank Thomas, Walter Crowell, Miss Alice Norwood, Mrs. Carrie Rudge Coble, Henry Brown, Dr. Redfern, Ed Austin, Will Rudge, Henry Walkup, unidentified man in doorway, Billy Benton. *Below*, The Monroe store today, built on the site of the first store

W. E. GALLANT, Anderson, South Carolina

GALLANT-BELK COMPANY, Winder, Georgia

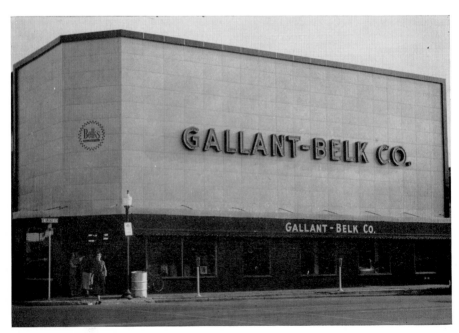

business in the hard times of the seventies. There were other farm boys in that community whose minds likewise had turned to the idea of becoming merchants, bankers, lawyers, manufacturers. The Belk brothers knew them from their boyhood days—many of them were kin by blood or marriage to the extensive Belk and Walkup families. It was natural that the Belks did not treat them simply as employees but as younger members of a large family connection needing advice and help—with a watchful eye to those who profited most by it. And it was natural that when the Belks began to set up stores in other towns, the men who headed them were not branch managers but younger partners in a family enterprise. There were many of these young men who started in the Monroe store. Prominent among them were John G. Parks, later to head the Parks-Belk groups of stores in Virginia and Tennessee; the Leggett brothers, who were to build up a group in Virginia and North Carolina; Karl Hudson, future head of the Belk-Hudson group, and Frank Stevens, of the Belk-Stevens group.

It was in this early period in Monroe that the Belk brothers took another step that was to become characteristic of their later policy. The first thousand dollars that they accumulated beyond the needs of their own organization they invested in the Monroe Cotton Mill, a new local enterprise in which their stock was a tenth interest. The Belks had watched with keen interest the growth of the cotton mills in the Piedmont —all along the lines of the railroad then known as the Richmond and Danville, from Danville, Virginia, through Charlotte, Spartanburg, South Carolina, to Atlanta, Georgia, the bustling new metropolis whose citizens were saying that it would soon be bigger than Richmond. A cotton mill looked like a good investment, and a local factory would have a payroll that would be good for a dry goods store doing a cash business. But beyond that the Belk brothers, with their experience of growing up and living in a farming community, did not need to be sold the gospel that men like Henry W. Grady were preaching—that the South would have to diversify its farming, and add manufacturing to farming, if it was ever to get on its feet again. Investment in diversified local industry and business was to become the fixed policy of the Belk organization and of the Belk brothers as individuals.

7

THE YEAR 1893 WAS ONE OF CRISIS FOR THE ENTIRE NA-
tion. The Belks were familiar with hard times for the farmer
—they had grown up with that—but by 1893 it was not
simply the cotton and tobacco farmers, but the wheat farmers
of the West as well. Out of hard times had grown the Farmers
Alliance, which in 1890 was headed by another North Carolinian, Leonidas L. Polk, and which boasted two million
members throughout the nation. Henry Belk was sympathetic
with their demand for free silver and easier credit to the
farmer, and although he did not join the Populist party when

it developed out of the Alliance in 1892, he did become an
"easy money" Democrat. In 1893 the chronic farm depression
was topped off by a business panic that threw the whole country into what was probably the worst general depression it
had ever suffered up to that time. All over the country banks,
railroads, manufacturing companies, and great mercantile
establishments were closing their doors. A real test of Henry
Belk's ideas and organization was at hand.

Under the test, the Belks found that the cash policy paid
off handsomely. They did not have the disagreeable job of
attempting to collect money where there was none. And
equally, since they paid their debts on a cash or short-term
basis, they did not have any distressed creditors pushing
them for money. And they discovered another thing—the
advantage of banking locally. They had used the Monroe
National Bank for all their business, and Colonel W. H.
Fitzgerald, then the cashier, had become a good friend and
admirer of the Belk way of doing business. Mr. Belk likes to
tell the story of what happened to a five thousand dollar loan
they negotiated through Colonel Fitzgerald at this time:

"The directors questioned the judgment of the cashier.
They said that was a lot of money to lend to a young man not
very long in business. It was a right smart lot of money in
those days. In fact, it's a lot of money nowadays.

"Well, Mr. Fitzgerald did not offer to argue with them.
He just went over to the vault, got out the note, and brought
it to them. Then he turned it over. His own signature was on
the back as indorsement. He had the money to back it, too.
But he never had to pay a cent on that note. Or any later one,
either."

The Belk brothers must have felt that their ideas were
sound, and they must have had an unshakable confidence in
themselves, for in the panic year of 1893, they did an extraor-

dinary thing. But there was nothing very dramatic about the way in which it happened.

One day Alex Kluttz of Chester, South Carolina, came into the store. He was the husband of Alice Jane Walkup, a first cousin of the brothers. For some time he had been in considerable difficulty financially. Henry Belk was somewhat surprised that young Kluttz seemed cheerful.

The two inquired about each other's health and the health of their various relatives, and then Mr. Belk asked his cousin by marriage how he was getting along.

"Well, Henry," young Kluttz replied, "as you know, I have been having it pretty tough lately. Things haven't been going good at all for me. As a matter of fact—" he looked Mr. Belk squarely in the eyes, and he was smiling—"I am completely stripped. I haven't got a cent in the world. But I don't owe anybody a cent either. It took all I had, but I'm even with the world. I'm in shape to start all over—at scratch."

A short time before this chance meeting between Mr. Belk and Mr. Kluttz, the Belks had bought the bankrupt stock of a store that had closed in Monroe. Now the idea suddenly occurred to Henry Belk to move this stock to Chester and with it set Alex Kluttz up in business. He had been impressed tremendously by his kinsman's attitude, his willingness and determination to pay his debts even though it took his last cent. Young Kluttz was honest. He had demonstrated that fact. And to Henry Belk that was the highest sort of recommendation. To his way of thinking, honesty was the first requisite.

They talked over the situation. Mr. Belk made Mr. Kluttz a proposition. It was accepted. The bankrupt store's stock was shipped to Chester and the Belk-Kluttz store opened for business.

"That's the way we started branching out," says Mr. Belk

in retrospect. "I had had no notion as a boy, or even after I had opened the store in Monroe, that I'd ever branch out. I guess we just fell into it. I just happened to be ready when a good proposition came along and I took it up. I suppose that's the way I have operated pretty much through the years. If a fellow is ready for an opportunity when it comes along, he can take advantage of it. I never did think much about this idea of luck. I figure that the fellow who is lucky is the one who is in position to take advantage of a good chance that comes along. In fact, he's the one who is in position to make the chance come along. We have never had any set policy about opening new stores and as a general thing they have turned out all right. We have had failures, of course, but usually we have had our judgment justified. When a young fellow develops into a good merchant and indicates to us that he is capable of running a store we usually are able to find a location for him and get him started out. Then it's pretty much up to him. We try to help him all we can, but it depends on him."

That was the first step in the Belk expansion. Given the times, it was venturesome—not to say daring. But it was not a wild leap into the dark. Henry Belk knew his man, and he also knew his region. Chester was only fifty miles away, across the border in South Carolina, and it was a town much like Monroe, in a farming community much like Union County. And it was the same with the store they set up next year, 1894, in Union, South Carolina, with Reece P. Harry as a co-owner and manager.

Nevertheless, the depression was getting worse rather than better. The Belks could keep up a good front about it, and Henry Belk could even have his private joke on the subject. Old friends of the two tell a story of a particular day when the brothers were standing on the sidewalk in front of their store. Henry Belk was near the curb, in shirt sleeves, snapping his suspenders. Dr. John was nearer the front door.

An acquaintance came by, spoke to the two, and turned to the older brother.

"Mr. Belk," he asked, "how's business?"

"Fine," replied Henry Belk, smiling and continuing to snap his suspenders. "Business is just fine."

The man, apparently a bit surprised at the answer, nodded and moved on down the street. When he was safely beyond hearing distance Dr. John confronted his brother.

"Brother Henry," he said, somewhat sadly, "that's the first time in my life I ever heard you tell a lie."

Henry Belk continued calmly to snap his suspenders.

"That was no lie, Brother John," he said, evenly and still smiling. "Business is fine, business is just fine, what you can get. In these days any business you can get is fine, yes sir, just fine."

But there was a jingle going around that pretty well summed up the feeling in the cotton country.

> Five cent cotton and ten cent meat—
> How in the devil can a poor man eat?

The Belks were keeping going, but it must have seemed to them that there would never be any real future in trying to run a store, or even a group of stores, in cotton country. They knew by now that they had a good idea and that they had enough seasoning and experience to make it work out. But they had both passed thirty and felt that the time had come to decide whether they would carry on as country merchants or try something bigger. At about this time the Monroe Cotton Mill, along with scores of others in the Piedmont, went into bankruptcy. The Belks could take the financial loss, but it was discouraging to see this first attempt to bring industry to the community go under. It was all the worse because some of the more conservative members of the community, who were down on the whole idea, were doing some gloating over the Belks' misfortune. Henry Belk began to look around.

He had been hearing interesting news from Texas. There was a new city out there, Houston, named for old Sam Houston, and according to all the reports Henry Belk had been able to get, Houston was growing fast and business was excellent. Money out there, these reports declared, was plentiful, and those big free-hearted Texans were eager to spend it.

So Henry Belk took the train for Houston.

In Houston he walked the streets, noticed that buildings were going up in almost every block, homes were being constructed. He went into the stores, examined the merchandise, inquired about prices. In spite of the depression, business seemed to be booming in the Texas city. Suits that he could purchase at from three dollars and fifty cents to four dollars were selling for sixteen dollars and fifty cents. And it seemed certain that Houston's growth would continue, that its expansion was being promoted on a solid basis. Houston was the center of a great and fast-growing empire. All factors of the community's life, as far as Henry Belk could determine it, indicated a most substantial future.

He was impressed. A great future for Belk Brothers Company, he foresaw, lay just ahead in Houston.

He caught the train home. He was tremendously excited when he reached Monroe. To Sarah Belk Simpson and Brother John he reported what he had found. He told them about four dollar suits that were selling for four times that amount. He outlined in glowing terms the marvelous development he had seen and how Houston held promise of even greater growth in the immediate future.

They would make money in Houston, he told them, and they would make it fast.

When he had finished talking, his mother spoke.

"Henry," she said, "it sounds like your chances out there

would be fine. I guess it's a good country for ambitious young men. A man coming up in a new country has a good chance of making a lot of money. I reckon you and John would get along fine.

"But it's a long way out to Texas, Henry. If you and John went out there to live it would be like telling you both good-bye for good. You might come home once a year, but it would be a long trip and it would cost you a lot of money. It wouldn't be long until you had lost most of your interest in this section of the country. And this is where your folks lived before you, and where you were born and brought up. I don't want you and John to go out there. I don't want you boys to leave me."

They did not. Their mother's words ended the Texas dream.

Henry Belk often tells of his Texas plans that never materialized. One day he was relating the story to a friend who had come to visit him in his handsome new office in the Belk's Buying Service building in Charlotte. In front of him on the roller-top desk lay the weekly trial balances of business done by each of the approximately three hundred Belk stores from Maryland to Texas and Ohio to Florida.

Mr. Belk laid the back of his hand on the sheets in a characteristic gesture, and smiled wryly.

"You know," he said, "I'm glad I didn't go out there to set myself up in business. My mother didn't want me and Brother John to go. She didn't want us to leave her, and she never would have consented to go out there to live. So we didn't go. And I'm glad we didn't.

"But I was right about Houston. It has grown to be a great city, and there's a lot of business and a lot of money out there. Look at that fellow Jesse Jones, for instance. You know if I had gone out there like I figured I would—" he hesitated, and his eyes twinkled above the rim of the spectacles on his nose—"I might have been a rich man today."

III

CITY MERCHANT

8

T HERE COULD HAVE BEEN MORE THAN A MOTHER'S LONGING
to have her sons near her in Sarah Belk Simpson's objection
to the Texas venture. She may have sensed that they would
be happier and even more successful in a business way if they
stayed closer to the region that they both knew so well. So
when Henry, who had made his decision and was not to be
denied his wish to try something bigger, suggested Charlotte as
a likely place, she was delighted. Charlotte was twenty-five
miles away—an hour on the train—and Henry could come
back for week ends. John would stay in Monroe—his second

daughter, Sadie, had been born in 1893, and he wanted to raise his family there—and take charge of the Monroe store. It would be easy enough for him to get to Charlotte when he was needed there, and the partnership could continue as close as it had been. It seemed a good solution to all three of them.

The city of Charlotte, North Carolina, could look back on a distinguished colonial and Revolutionary War history, but in 1895 its citizens were much less inclined to dwell upon the glories of its past than the promise of its future. The panic of 1893 had been a setback, and a sharp one, but it had not dimmed the hopes of Charlotte. Since before the Civil War it had been the hub of developing railroads, and in the seventies and eighties it found itself in a key spot on the Richmond and Danville Railroad, which had consolidated many short lines to create a system giving through service from Washington and Richmond to Atlanta. The Richmond and Danville had been a victim of the panic, but in 1894 J. P. Morgan had reorganized it as the Southern Railway, the largest railroad system in the southeast.

Along the Southern Railway, from Danville, Virginia, to Atlanta, were the cotton mills, and by 1895 they were consuming 40 per cent as much cotton as the northern mills. Optimists in Charlotte were saying that the day would come when the South would be ahead of New England. In 1895 North Carolina alone had nearly 1,000,000 spindles and 25,000 looms in operation—in 1870 there had been 40,000 spindles and 600 looms. Set in the middle of all this development, Charlotte felt itself destined to be not only a big manufacturing city, but a center for banking, insurance, and merchandising. It had already outgrown Raleigh, the state capital, and in North Carolina it was second only to Wilmington. Its actual population of fifteen thousand was no measure of the confidence it felt in the future, or its feeling of being a real city.

The Charlotte merchants knew of the Belk brothers and their success in Union County but did not feel that it meant anything by city standards. Joseph Baruch, an uncle of Bernard Baruch and one of the leading merchants of the time, was heard to remark that "those Belk boys may be good country-town merchants, but they won't last six months in Charlotte." (It was a special pleasure to the Belks to buy out Mr. Baruch's stock when he went out of business later in the decade.) There was little fear and some merriment among the Charlotte merchants at the Belks' plans.

Henry Belk had picked the location—a store on the first block of East Trade Street. It was half again as big as the Monroe store but nothing great by Charlotte standards. The store opened on September 25, 1895.

Henry Belk had no intention of changing any of the methods of operation that he had tested and proved in Monroe. His line would be bigger because Charlotte had more varied needs, but he was not after the luxury trade. He was after the ordinary man and woman who wanted the economy that went with paying cash, the insurance that went with the policy of complete freedom in returning goods, and the satisfaction that went with quick and courteous service.

The Belk policy worked. The depression made things harder in some ways, but it also had the effect of making people price conscious, and the Belk way of doing business had been worked out for the price-conscious farmers of Union County. The townspeople of Charlotte found it equally attractive. Belk Brothers Company—the corporate name they chose—did not leap overnight to the place of leadership, but it was on its feet within a surprisingly short time. Within a year Henry Belk was buying out the stock of another store, T. L. Alexander & Company, and in the process learning a lesson that was to become another Belk policy. He needed ten thousand dollars to finance the transaction, and the Charlotte National Bank, to which he went first, demanded a mortgage. He went down to Monroe to discuss it with his brother, but Mrs. John Belk became worried over signing away her dower interest. The brothers hesitated, then decided they were not going to distress their womenfolk by signing mortgages. Henry Belk went back to Charlotte and told the bank that he and his brother would never sign a mortgage for operating credit—only for buying and improving real property. The Belks have followed that policy to this day.

But again the Belks found a banker who trusted them— this time it was J. M. Miller, then cashier of the Merchants and Farmers National Bank. He later became president of the First and Merchants Bank of Richmond and Governor of the Federal Reserve Bank of Richmond. Mr. Miller was agreeable to a loan, the deal went through, and Belk Brothers Company was able to repay it quickly.

The recollections of an old friend of the Belks, Mr. B. L. Scruggs of Charlotte, give a warm and revealing picture of the Belks and Charlotte storekeeping practices at this period. Mr. Scruggs says:

"My position in those days was cashier of what I believe was Charlotte's first department store, and it was Mr. Belk's principal competitor as he was getting started. It was the old W. J. Davis & Company, known then as the 'Racket Store.' It employed 105 salespersons, too, and was certainly no small establishment for a town of that size.

"Storekeeping in those times was hard work. It meant long hours, being on the job from seven in the morning until eight, nine, and ten o'clock on week days and until eleven and almost twelve on Saturday nights from September through Christmas.

"I used to eat at the old Central Hotel, and Mr. Henry Belk frequently sat with me. He lived in a room over his store, but he took his meals at the Central, which had the best

Belk's Department Store, West Palm Beach, Florida

Matthews-Belk Company, Gastonia, North Carolina

K. G. HUDSON, Raleigh, North Carolina

HUDSON-BELK COMPANY, Raleigh, North Carolina (*credit Haynes' Studio*)

food in town. That was when you really got good things to eat at a hotel. I don't remember just how much we paid for board, but I think it was around four or five dollars a week for all three meals, and maybe less. And in those days they were meals. Chicken and country ham and fish and pork and beef, mutton, lamb, partridges, duck, geese, turkey. And all sorts of vegetables—and right fresh, too—and pies and cakes, hot biscuits, honey, jam and jelly. It was really fine eating back then.

"Quite often Dr. John M. Belk, Mr. Henry Belk's brother, would be at the table with us. Dr. John was running the Belk store in Monroe and Mr. Henry was running the one in Charlotte. I was impressed with the devotion the two men had for each other; in fact, I don't think I have ever seen two brothers, especially grown men, more attached to each other than the two Belks.

"They were both rather tender-hearted, too, and it showed up in a peculiar way. Sometimes Dr. John would show up at our table and Mr. Henry would be missing. We figured then that Mr. Henry had gone out of town on business and had called in Dr. John to look after the store while he was away. Mr. Henry often went to New York and Baltimore and other places up north and east on buying trips and during those times he had a habit of calling in Dr. John to take charge of the Charlotte store.

"But it wasn't always for that reason. Every now and then it became necessary for Mr. Henry or Dr. John to fire one of the clerks. Not often, for the Belk store personnel seemed to get along mighty well and the clerks seemed satisfied, but every now and then. And the way the Belks went about it was sort of funny, I always thought. Mr. Henry, I remember especially, just didn't like to fire folks, even when he had to do it. So he'd usually leave town for a few days after telling Dr. John to come up to Charlotte. While he was away Dr. John would fire the fellow and then Mr. Henry would come back home and Dr. John would return to Monroe. And sometimes they did it the other way around. Dr. John would call Mr. Henry to Monroe to fire one of the clerks in the Monroe store while he was away, perhaps up here in Charlotte. But there wasn't much firing done, as I recall. The Belks were known as easy people to get along with.

"I well remember another characteristic of the Belk brothers that made a great impression upon me, and that was the great devotion they had for their mother. They always referred to her with the most evident respect and veneration. It was an inspiration to everybody who knew them, and I have always had a feeling that it must have had something to do with the great success they made of their business.

"Mr. Henry would sit with us on warm summer evenings for a while after we'd had our supper, but usually he wouldn't be there long before he'd excuse himself and get back to the store. Many was the time he would go back to the store after it had closed for the night and spend a couple of hours checking over the stock and getting the merchandise arranged in attractive style for the trade the next day, or working on his books and getting out orders for more merchandise. He was a working man—he just seemed to love to work, and that was his amusement, I suppose—and then, too, he didn't have any family to go home to and he didn't seem to be the least interested in the girls. In fact, I always had the idea that around the womenfolks, unless he was selling them some piece goods or something else from the store, he was downright shy. Most of the young fellows— and he wasn't so young in those days, either, for he was in his thirties—would hire rigs from the livery stable and take their girls for rides on summer nights and Sunday afternoons, but not Mr. Belk. I don't recall ever seeing him out courting.

He put in most of his time, when he wasn't sleeping or eating, at the store."

One of the things not mentioned by Mr. Scruggs that the bachelor merchant was doing in the store at night was writing advertising copy. The Belk policy of a small profit on the unit sale would not work unless it produced a big volume. Competition was much fiercer in Charlotte than it had been in Monroe—other merchants from the country had picked Charlotte as a good location and were trying their luck there. From the beginning the Belks believed in advertising. In a day when merchants buy page after page of newspaper advertising and keep the air lanes jammed with flattering descriptions of what they have to offer, it would seem only natural that a merchant should advertise lavishly the merchandise he is seeking to sell. But a half century ago, advertising, like the electric railway cars that on May 20, 1894, succeeded the horse-drawn cars in Charlotte, was considered by many to be an unnecessary innovation.

But not everybody regarded it so. Already another North Carolinian, W. T. Blackwell of Durham, had used the figure of a bull to give world-wide fame not only to his tobacco but to his home town. And the Dukes were also astounding the country by the novel advertising methods they used to push the products of their newly organized American Tobacco Company. The Belks definitely belonged to the liberal wing regarding advertising. The advertisements were novel, judged by the standards of present day copy-writers, but they had a spontaneity and engaging informality that must have caused them to be highly effective, for they were widely read and they evidently aided greatly in bringing in the customers.

It was long before the day of advertising specialists on the staffs of business houses, nor were the newspapers in position to offer their advertisers highly specialized aid. A merchant had something to sell; he bought some space in the newspaper and told what he had and the price. That was his ad. It is still the basic form of newspaper advertisements, but today they seek to come upon the customer in a devious way; they employ what the advertising agencies very learnedly call psychology. Perhaps some of the Belk ads a half century ago did the same thing and perhaps at times more effectively, but they made no pretense of being clever.

"I used to write the ads myself," Mr. Belk recalls. "I'd usually do it at night after the store was closed. I'd look over my new stock and get a pretty good idea of what I had that would be good to mention in the ad, and then I'd write it down. And they ran it just as I wrote it."

Frequently the same copy would be run for an entire week. The policy of running a different advertisement each day, designed to sell a particular group of articles being offered for sale that day—or the next day if the ad were being carried in the afternoon daily—would be a development of later years. The advertisement, whether it was always effective or not in doing a specific selling job, served to keep the name of "Belk Bros., Cheapest Store on Earth, 15 to 21 East Trade St.," always before the public.

An advertisement written by Mr. Belk and published in 1897, two years after the Charlotte store was opened, reveals not only what the store had to sell at that time, but also the downright confidence of the Belks in their ability to outdistance their competitors.

Under a large-type heading "BELK BROS." at the top of a two-column by six-inch display—which in those days was a large ad—Mr. Belk wrote:

HERE WE COME; SOMEBODY HEAD US

No doubt this cry has often been raised in this portion of the vineyard, but, brother, we came here to do the business of Charlotte and all the combinations that can be mustered up, together with the aid of Uncle Sam and the Home Guard thrown in, cannot even check us.

GET THERE, YOU BET.

Yes, with the cargo of Boots, Shoes, Clothing, Dry Goods, Notions, Hats, etc., just landed, we are prepared to do up the town in short order; so get out of the way or you will be run over by the thousands pressing in upon us. We are here for business, and don't you forget it. Why it is worth tramping a hundred miles or two to see the biggest concern in either of the Carolinas, and to watch the throngs of eager buyers as they file in and out of the Gigantic Establishment. Others try to imitate our example in many ways, but they haven't got the "get up and get" about them. Too far out of sight to ever get a glimpse of what is going on in the arena. Buying up a bankrupt stock or a panic merchant, and selling the same out in a few days, completely demoralizes some folks. We don't believe in charging regular prices for goods bought up in this way—just add our one little short profit and stop, and let 'er go, gallagher. This accounts for the big crowds we always have for the people know where to come to get special bargains. Just closed out a nice clean stock of Gents' Furnishing Goods; also a splendid line of Sample Shirts, Underwear, Half Hose, Ties, Bows, Hats, etc., at half price. Scriven Drawers only 68c.; who ever heard of such a thing? And, my, the hundreds of cases of Boots, Shoes, Clothing, Dry Goods, Hats, Notions, etc., that are piling in from Bunker Hill and New York settlements. If you want to feel like you are on one of the great thoroughfares just stand in front of our three stores and watch the jam almost any day, and you will decide this must be a second Broadway. Of course, we are the only attraction on Trade Street, as you will observe. Watch out for our signs and don't be side-tracked, for we are the only original

BELK BROTHERS

Cheapest Store on Earth   15 to 21 East Trade Street

Equal confidence in themselves, together with the kind of political comment that fitted the times, is shown by another Belk advertisement of that period. It is also a commentary on the tough competitive conditions of that era, when a sharp eye for the values in the stock of a bankrupt competitor or manufacturer was a most important business asset. This advertisement is headed by the name of the President:

PRESIDENT McKINLEY

Says up. Hanna says down. Reed says wiggle, waggle. To a man up a tree this is about the situation as it stands at the capital. Unsettled condition of the country. Very different in the commercial world. Why look at

BELK BROS.

They have forever scattered to the four winds high prices and big profits, settled this matter without the assistance of any government. No unrest now among the masses of this section. Thousands walk up to this fountain of low prices and all go away refreshed and invigorated by coming in contact with the healing properties of our dispensary. Your pocket-book will be tickled and the waste places that have been made desolate by ravages of the credit system will soon blossom as the rose by sticking to us. The same spirit of

INDEPENDENCE

that filled our forefathers with enthusiasm on the 20th of May, 1775, will be imparted to you by simply visiting our gigantic establishment. Congress nor any other power have any right to step in and regulate prices. We are the sole owners of our various stores throughout the country and by buying in such tremendous quantities we can afford to very often sell goods at half price or less than manufacturers' cost. Of course it takes the hard cash to carry on business successfully. Frequently we close out a hard-pressed manufacturer of his entire lot and almost every day we are in receipt of letters from different sections of this Union offering us bankrupt stocks, etc., at often less than 50 cents on the dollar. No trouble for us to scoop them in, for we always have the wherewith on hand. Think of it: Selling 21 yards of the best 4-4 bleaching for $1, as good as the Fruit of Loom or other standard brands. Barker Mills 4-4 at same price. Alamance, 2½c, calico, 2½c, lawns, 2½c, Turkey red calico, 2½c, 10c and 12½c; percales, the best, only 5c, silk for shirt waists worth 75c, going at 48c. Hundreds of ready-made skirts, and shirt waists being turned out by us at prices that will astonish you. Our clothing stock is attracting every passer by. $5 suits displayed in show window cannot be touched with a forty-foot pole. Knobbiest line of clothing that ever hit Mecklenburg grit. Thousands of pairs of ladies' Oxford ties and slippers in all colors, widths, toes, etc., just in. Work shirt, 10c; undershirt, 10c; unlaundered shirt, 18c; half hose, 2½c. Each of the following articles

ONE CENT

24 sheets of paper, 2 boxes blacking, cake soap, 25 marbles, 13 pens, 7 pen holders, 25 envelopes, 2 key rings, 12 lead pencils, 2 boxes blueing, 2 fishing lines, 15 fish hooks, paper hooks and eyes, 1 pipe, 2 blank books, 4 boxes matches, 2 balls thread, handkerchief, yard ribbon, 200 yards spool cotton, and thousands of other useful articles at same price. Turn loose the limb and come in a sweeping gallop to

BELK BROS.

Cheapest Store on Earth   15 to 21 East Trade Street

But perhaps most important in the Belk advertising was its continued insistence on how much could be obtained for a little money. This line reached its climax in an advertisement headed simply

THE PURCHASE POWER OF ONE "BROWNIE"

followed by this list of its offerings:

Two yards Ribbon for 1c.
One nice Fold Fan, 1c.
Two Cakes Soap for 1c.
Two Papers Needles for 1c.
One Paper Gold-Eyed Needles, 1c.
One Paper No. 2½ Safety Pins, 1c.
One pair Side Combs, 1c.
One Paper Pins, 1c.
Three Jack-Stones, 1c.
Two Aluminum Hairpins, 1c.
One card Hooks and Eyes, 1c.
One Tape Line, 1c.
Two Lead Pencils, 1c.
Ten Pen Staffs, 1c.
One small Looking Glass, 1c.
Six black Hat Pins for 1c.
Six Pen Points for 1c.
One Pocketbook, 1c.
Two pairs Shoe Strings, 1c.
One pair Tubular Shoe Laces, 1c.
Two papers Carpet Tacks, 1c.
Twenty-eight Marbles for 1c.
Two balls Sewing Thread, 1c.
One 200 yard Spool Thread, 1c.
One spool Linen Thread, 1c.

One Top, 1c.
Eight Fish Hooks, 1c.
Three boxes Matches, 1c.
Two Teaspoons, 1c.
One Shoe Brush, 1c.
Two Fish Lines, 1c.
One Pipe with Stem, 1c.
One Jews Harp, 1c.
Two Lamp Wicks, 1c.
One yard Lace, 1c.
One Yard Embroidery, 1c.
Two packs Hairpins, 1c.
Three Collar Buttons, 1c.
Twenty-five Envelopes for 1c.
Two Shoe Hooks, 1c.
One Beats-All Pencil, 1c.
Three dozen Agate Buttons for 1c.
Six Knitting Needles, 1c.
One box black Mourning Pins, 1c.
One Man's White Necktie, 1c.
One finger Ring, 1c.
One King Collar Button, 1c.
One roll No. 4 or 6 Tape, 1c.
Two yards Soutache Braid, 1c.
One Pencil Sharpener, 1c.
One box good Bluing, 1c.

Nor was Henry Belk content to proclaim to the world through the newspapers that Belk Brothers was the cheapest store on earth. Fifty years ago the mountaineers often came down from the Blue Ridge and the Great Smokies to peddle their wares from their long covered wagons. After they had sold out their apples—and some times an occasional drop or two of a more liquid product of their orchards and cornfields —they would drive around to Belk Brothers to lay in a stock of ginghams, calicoes, brogans, and other merchandise. Mr. Belk often would throw in an extra bolt of cloth or a kitchen utensil or a pair of lines in return for the privilege of having a sign placed upon the side of the wagon. The sign in flaming large letters would advise all who saw the returning covered wagon that "It Pays to Trade at Belk Bros., Cheapest Store on Earth."

And they tell further—and have a photograph to prove it —that once Mr. Belk had two large signs painted that proclaimed in big letters:

BELK's
For the Best
SHOE
Values
in Town
THIS IS NO BULL

They had the signs sandwiched across the back of a large-uddered cow which was then led through the streets of the city by a straw-hatted farmer with a milk pail on his arm.

9

I‍T IS INTERESTING TO PICTURE BELK BROTHERS COMPANY as it operated around the turn of the century—before automobiles, the movies, and the radio had revolutionized the American way of life. There are old-timers in the organization who can give the details—people like B. Frank Matthews, a Mecklenburg boy who got his first job with Mr. Belk in 1898 "cleaning old wool hats" and rose to become manager of the Charlotte store and head of the men's clothing department of the central buying office; Miss Sarah Houston, who joined the organization in 1900, just as the store was installing a millinery department, and eventually became a departmental buyer; or Lem Whitsett, now an official in an engraving firm in Charlotte, who as a check-boy in those days saw the organization from a special inside position.

The business day would open with the check-boys—real jacks of all trade—sweeping the floors and taking the tarpaulins off the counters. That would be well before seven in the morning because the store opened then. Also before seven, bolts of cloth and other merchandise especially enticing to the public were taken outside and put on wooden stands against the store front. Still another inducement to the public was—in summer time—a big barrel of ice water in the entrance, with a large sign, FREE ICE WATER, and five tin cups tied to it by a long string. A man would be posted at the front to steer in the hesitant customer. Frequently it was Henry Belk himself—he enjoyed hailing friends or acquaintances, inquiring about church affairs, talking about the special bargains of the day, and reminding customers of the free clock or watch that went with every suit of clothes. Inside was the orderly confusion of a busy store—the big bolts of yard goods on the left, men's suits in the center—not hung on racks but folded neatly on counters—shoes on the right. Through an arched opening was the women's department—dresses, blankets, sheets, and household furnishing; millinery was still another. The millinery department of that day was a world of its own, according to Miss Houston, and even Mr. Belk with his fondness for being all over the shop at once, did not often venture in. More hats were made to order than bought readymade, and what with the problem of their size and elaboration and fitting them safely over the pompadour of the day, each hat was truly a creation. But then as now women bought the wrong hats in spite of Miss Houston's arguments, spent days making up their minds and then wanted everything finished in a day, and men spent their time deploring the whole hat situation.

If it were fall there would be heavy business with the staple merchandise—farmers would be in town with their crop money, "buying up" at Belks for maybe a year's needs. If it were spring and just before Easter, Miss Houston's millinery department would be swamped, and the girls there would work far into the night to make the hats in time. Throughout the year there would be special sales of one sort or another, depending on what Henry Belk had found in New York or Baltimore or picked up at the liquidation of a manufacturer or another mercantile house.

There was little mail-order business, and not even the telephone was used to any extent. People wanted to see what they got—and besides, with the few forms of entertainment then available, shopping about was the most fun that most people had. So all day long the check-boys would be on the run, taking merchandise from the clerk who had made the sale to the wrapping counter under the cashier's cage, then the wrapped package back to the clerk or customer, with the change.

There was no regular hour for closing. But some time between seven and eight—later on Saturdays—someone would stroll out on the sidewalk and look up and down. "Carolina Clothing Company's closing. So is Efird's. Maybe we just as well." At closing time Mr. Belk himself paid off the check-boys—twenty-five cents for a day's work. It was easier to keep accounts that way, and also Henry Belk wanted the chance to pass on a word of commendation or a small bonus. There were future top executives among them. Even after the payoff, however, the check-boys' day might not be done, because the delivery men needed their help for late deliveries.

Mr. Whitsett, the former check-boy, recalls with special

affection a Negro delivery man with whom he frequently shared nighttime adventure.

"Everybody called him 'Speck,'" Mr. Whitsett reveals. "He was a light brown fellow with freckles all over his face. Speck drove the delivery wagon for me. We'd drive up to the address, and I'd get out and deliver the package. We'd carry a lantern and often I had to get out and try to locate the house number with the help of the flickering light from that old lantern. Sometimes we had a lot of trouble finding the right house, and many a time I had a dog bite me while I was fumbling around looking for the address we were trying to find. Many a night, especially around Christmas time, we would be ten and eleven o'clock getting through making our deliveries. And after that we had to take the wagon back to the stable, unhitch the horse, rub him down, and feed him."

Mr. Whitsett also remembers vividly how Henry Belk appeared to a check-boy working for him.

"He didn't seem to mind work. In fact, Mr. Henry seemed to get a lot of pleasure out of selling things. He was all over the store seeing to anything he might be needed for. If a lot of customers came in and all the clerks were busy, he'd pitch in and start selling things himself. I think he actually liked to get an excuse to wait on customers. He always carried a small pair of scissors in his vest pocket—they tell me he still does—and when a lady bought two or three yards of piece goods—it was usually more than that, though, for skirts were full and long in those days—he'd snip the cloth where his measuring had come out, and then with a swish he would tear it across. Or he might help wait on a man who was figuring on buying a suit of clothes or shirts or underwear or socks or shoes. He always seemed to want to sell a man or a woman something that the customer really wanted, and he always wanted them to feel that they had made a good trade. Not many people brought stuff back, and when they did Mr. Henry wouldn't argue with them. He'd take the returned article and give back the money without turning a word. I think that was one of the principal reasons for the great success of the Belk stores. It was the policy at Belk's always to please the customer and make him want to come back for more purchases."

Henry Belk's day lasted longer than even that of the latest check-boy. Just because he wanted to be on the floor as much as possible during the day, and felt he was needed to set an example of courtesy, to handle problems on the spot, to make all the workers feel that he was with them, he had to put off until night the other tasks that were equally essential to running the store—checking inventory, planning new arrangements of stock, writing up orders, writing advertisements, studying his accounts. With all his vitality, it must have been a tired man who took the train down to Monroe on Sunday— as he did every week that he was not out of town—to see his mother, to talk things over with his brother, and to get a bit of relaxation with John's growing children.

IV

MERCHANT OF THE CAROLINAS

Dr. JOHN M. BELK shortly before his death

WILLIAM HENRY BELK at the age of thirty-five

J. G. PARKS, Johnson City, Tennessee

PARKS-BELK COMPANY, Maryville, Tennessee

10

A S THE CENTURY DREW TO A CLOSE, THE BELK BROTHERS could look with satisfaction on what they had achieved as city merchants. They had worked hard, and at times they had felt pushed close to the wall, but they had proved that their way of doing business would work, in the toughest times and with the sharpest kind of competition. Belk Brothers was now an acknowledged leader among Charlotte's dry goods stores. Already it had expanded by leasing space on the adjoining property, and there had been articles in Charlotte papers acclaiming the Belks' success, complimenting them on their polite and efficient service. They had made themselves liked among their customers, whether they were country people who came in once or twice a year to stock up, or townspeople dropping in every week to see what Belk's had to offer.

They could also feel that they had maintained a fine spirit among the people who worked for them. Belk's in Charlotte was known among its competitors as an outfit with a high morale—a good place for a steady job. On a recent Thanksgiving day the Belks had taken the whole Charlotte crowd down to Monroe for a dinner with the Monroe crowd at Dr. John Belk's big new house. There had been over a hundred guests, and it had been like a big family gathering. There was nothing unusual about that, because so many of them were from the Waxhaws themselves, like the Belks, and some were family connections. The Belks knew they were liked and admired by the people they were closest to.

And they had been right in picking Charlotte. It was not too easy to pick the right town in that period, because with all the railroad consolidations that were going on a town that seemed to have a great future might find itself sitting on a branch line ten years later. But the formation of the Southern Railway had been decisive, and Charlotte was in a key position on it, halfway between Washington and Atlanta. It was nearing twenty thousand in population, with many thousands more in the immediate area, and new factories were opening, new businesses being established, new people moving in. Charlotte set its sights high.

The worst of the depression was over. Farm prices were still low, but they were rising—a period was being ushered in that would be taken thirty years later as the standard for "parity" in the relation between farm and industrial prices. The political battles of the earlier nineties were being forgotten, and many of the old wounds of the Civil War had been healed in the common effort of the war with Spain.

"McKinley prosperity" was beginning to be talked about, even in the South—and in truth the South had made enormous strides in the twenty-five years since Reconstruction ended. With its cotton mills in the Piedmont, its tobacco factories in North Carolina, Virginia, and Kentucky, its iron and coal in Tennessee and Alabama, and with new crops like peanuts, apples, and peaches, and truck farming in various sections, it was beginning to look a little like the land that the Henry Gradys hoped it would be. North Carolina was sharing heavily in this development, with its textile mills and tobacco factories, and in the nineties it had added a whole new industry in the furniture manufacturing plants that centered around Greensboro and High Point. The Belks may have wondered still what might have happened if they had gone to Texas, but they could not be unhappy that they had stayed in North Carolina.

It would have been easy—and perhaps there was a temptation—for them to make Charlotte the last step, to expand with that growing community, to consolidate their position as leading local merchants. The other three stores could be kept going as an evidence of their early work, and the Charlotte store could be made the final achievement. It would have been a respectable and highly successful career for two country boys turned merchants. If you ask Mr. Belk today why this was not the case, he will say simply that he liked merchandising too much ever to want to limit his field, that opportunities were always turning up, and that there was always developing somewhere in his organization some young man who looked like a promising junior partner. Besides, he believed so strongly in his idea of good merchandising so much that he wanted to prove it everywhere he could.

That is a large part of the answer to the question—in the character of the man. Confidence in the future, the willingness to take risk on a business transaction or on a man, was part of his nature. It became a cardinal point of his and his brother's teaching, which all of their associates emphasize, that a merchant should never talk hard times. This optimism was not feigned. The Belks knew it was good business to talk good times and write good times in their advertising copy, but they were actually and in a very real sense optimists. Henry Belk at nearly eighty-eight is still an optimist. Better times, he is confident, are always just ahead. He has never reached a point where he looks back to the virtues of the past or ahead to a civilization going to the dogs.

Confidence in his merchandising ideas was another reason for wanting to go ahead. He belonged to the second generation of American merchants who were transforming the country store into the modern department store. John Wanamaker and Marshall Field had been the first generation. They had pioneered in Philadelphia and Chicago with cash, the one-price system, and the policy of full returns, eliminating the traditional bargaining over the counter and thus enabling merchandising to be put on a mass basis. At the turn of the century they were probably the leading houses in the country, and Henry Belk is always quick to point out that he learned a good part of his philosophy from watching their practice. He may well have thought that in a region like the South, still largely rural and small town, only some grouping of stores over a wide area would allow him to put new merchandising ideas across.

In Henry Belk's own generation of American merchants were the men who were going to perfect the dominant methods of modern merchandising. As the new century came in F. W. Woolworth was beginning to find his five-and-ten stores in New York and Pennsylvania working out successfully. As long ago as 1872 Montgomery Ward had put out his first catalogue—a leaflet—and by the time Henry Belk set up his own store in Monroe, Ward was publishing a 150-page catalogue and doing a million dollar business. And in 1895 Julius Rosenwald, who was the same age as Henry Belk, agreed to become vice president of a small business in Chicago which had just changed its name from R. W. Sears Watch Company to Sears, Roebuck and Company. The chain store and the national mail-order house were on their way.

In New York City about 1900, Isidor Straus had only recently taken over full control of R. H. Macy and Co. and was setting out to make it the world's biggest single department store. And in Boston, the Filene brothers, who had formed a partnership to take over the business their father left them in the same year that the Belk brothers became partners, were also introducing those merchandising methods that were to make their establishment famous.

But the Belks were to develop neither as a great single store nor as a chain or mail-order house. The southeast had no metropolis big enough to be the base for a single enormous store, and something in their own character and background kept them from setting up a chain. It is interesting to note that all of the merchants just mentioned except the Filenes started their business ventures in locations far from where they had been reared. But the Belks never really left home— Union County, the Waxhaws, Charlotte. The intense family feeling that they inherited from their widowed mother remained with them and was reflected in their business ideas and in their attitude toward the people working under them. All of this led them to develop a system of stores that would turn out to be something new in the field of merchandising. It would have the spread and reach of a chain and would possess many of the operational assets of a great chain system, but it would be distinctly not a chain; it would permit the individual store to be an individual and to develop its own personality. It would be like a big Union County family, with the father as the source of final authority, but with the individual children allowed and encouraged to grow up and be themselves and have families of their own.

The Belks would hardly have put it in this way if in those early days they were setting out to describe their system. The Belk way of organization could not have been planned in advance because it depended on too many human factors. The Belks were feeling their way. Actually, during the period from the beginning of the century to the opening of the First World War, the number of new stores added was not large, and all of them were within a hundred miles of Charlotte. Mr. Belk's own description of the expansion in that period gives an indication of how the Belk idea was developing:

"It was in 1899 that we opened up in Greensboro. Times were still a little tight but we figured Greensboro was a good place for a new store, and it proved out that we were right. It was a good town and still is. We're doing a good volume of business in Greensboro.

"Two years later we opened up another store, which was our sixth. We put J. H. Matthews in business over there in Gastonia. He is one of the Matthews boys who has been with us a long time, way back since the early days of the business. He's one of the boys from down in the Providence section that we trained in our way of doing business. We've got a lot of men like him who came up in the Belk stores. And they're good merchants, too."

The year after the launching of the Matthews-Belk Company at Gastonia, the seventh store, the Belk-Harry Company, was established in Salisbury. That was in 1902.

"Well, we ran along that way for a good while before we opened up any more stores. We just tried to push along with those we were already running. Then in 1910 we started a store at Sanford. That was in January, and the next month we opened up another store at York, South Carolina, which in those days they called Yorkville. Then in 1911 we went into

Concord, and a couple of years later we set up in Statesville. "That's the way it went. We weren't trying to build up any big system of stores. We just took advantage of what we considered good opportunities in towns that we figured would be good places for locating our stores. We would have a smart, aggressive young fellow, ambitious to move along and do better than he was doing as a clerk, who would want to start out for himself. Well, when we had one like that, we'd back him. Maybe he had saved up a little money that he could put into the business. We'd lend him some more to put into it and we'd put up some ourselves. Or we'd arrange it so that he could buy stock and pay for it as he made the money.

"That's how we came to have a group of Belk stores. When we found out we had such a young man in one of our stores, we'd get a proposition worked out and then we'd buy a stock of merchandise, rent or buy a stand, and he'd open up for business."

A study of location of the stores is revealing. Greensboro, Salisbury, Concord, Gastonia—these cities were on the main line of the Southern, north and south of Charlotte, and all were growing industrial towns. Greensboro, which was to become one of the biggest stores in the Belk system, was near the center of the new furniture manufacturing business. Near Concord was the Cannon Mills, which was on its way to becoming one of the giants in the textile business. Gastonia was in the county that was to have the largest number of textile mills in North Carolina. York and Statesville were just off the axis of the railroad. Only Sanford, in central North Carolina, was a town reminiscent of the Monroe that the Belks started from —a trading center for cotton and tobacco farmers. The Belks were shrewd in their choice of locations.

In a small group, such as the Belk stores were at this time, problems of organization were simple—that is, relative to what they would become. The stores were separately incorporated, and the brothers divided between themselves the roles of president and vice president of each store, and held the majority of stock. Usually the manager and co-owner would be secretary and treasurer. But even at this early date the Belk idea was given emphasis in the names of the stores, which were not all named simply Belk's or Belk Brothers or Belk's Department Store. There might have been advertising value in holding the one name of Belk before the public— capitalizing on the success in Charlotte. The developing chain stores were handling their expansions in just this way.

But that would not give the younger manager and co-owner the right kind of break. He should be allowed to have his name before the community in which he was settling; he should be permitted and encouraged to develop the special personality of his store. Even at this early date, the Belks were almost instinctively diverging from the main line of multiple-store development toward a system of their own. Thus, the store at Gastonia was the Matthews-Belk Company, the one at Salisbury the Belk-Harry Company, the one at Sanford the Williams-Belk Company, the one at Greensboro the Belk-Brown Company—only later it was changed to its present name.

Buying trips in New York and Baltimore were like family affairs. Each store sent its own buyer to select for its own needs, but they usually went north in a group, after talking things over with Mr. Henry and Dr. John in Charlotte. Often Henry Belk went along to buy for the Charlotte store and to advise—not to dictate to—the other buyers on the goods offered. The Charlotte store was much the largest purchaser, and in many lines of merchandise the prices he could get were better than the other buyers could obtain. In addition, frequently he could deal directly with the textile mills and other manufacturing concerns in the purchase of large quantities of goods. In a perfectly natural way the Charlotte store soon had become a distributing point and stock room for all the stores in the group. The group thereby was able to get the benefit of large-order prices without sacrificing individual initiative. This would give each individual store a tremendous advantage over its local competition.

11

THE STORES CONTINUED TO BE THE TRAINING GROUNDS FOR future Belk leaders. At the Charlotte store there were the Matthews brothers from Mecklenburg County—five of them in all. One had already been sent to operate the Gastonia store. Another—actually the first of the family to join Belk Brothers— was B. Frank Matthews, and he was to become manager of the Charlotte store and later a buyer in the buying agency for the Belk group. Later another brother, W. M. (Mack) Matthews, and two half-brothers, Henry B. Matthews, and Oliver Matthews, were to get Belk training and rise to executive positions in the organization. Frank Matthews has this to say about his early days at the Charlotte store:

"Mr. Henry put me to work cleaning old wool hats. That was the first job he gave me. Later I had the job of cleaning the tinware and other merchandise in that general line. Then for a while I was check-boy and later cashier; in fact, I suppose I have done about everything there is to do around a store. It has been a long time since I started cleaning old hats for Mr. Henry. In that time I have seen the Belk organization grow into a vast system, and I have been in it almost from the start.

"It has moved out like a fish-net; I believe that is the way to picture its growth. Mr. Belk is always developing young men who open other stores. And they are all trained in the Belk methods of doing business, so that although the stores as they are opened are independent establishments they are at the same time similar in their ways of doing business and in their adherence to the same general principles of doing business.

"For instance, I well remember giving W. E. Gallant his first job. It was back in 1906. He was a hard-working young man and I remember that he soon became an expert in silks and woolens. Mr. Henry Belk and Dr. John Belk had a high regard for him, and he was very well liked by the customers, too. After the Belk organization began to expand, the Belks made him a proposition to open a store at Anderson, S. C. He went down there and opened up, worked hard and used his brains, and now he's head of the big Gallant-Belk subgroup of some thirty-five stores. He's an example of what many young men who were willing to work and had smart merchandising heads were able to do through the cooperation of the Belks. And he's an example, too, of the ability the Belks had in spotting promising young men and through encouragement and wise counsel developing them into first-rate merchants."

Mr. Gallant himself entertainingly gives this description of the kind of training he received:

"I went to work in the Charlotte store when I was seventeen years old. That was back in 1906. That's a long time and much has happened in merchandising in that time, and the Belk stores have expanded into a tremendous merchandising system that does a great volume of business. I was put in what they then described as the piece goods section. I helped sell all types of cotton goods, blankets, comforts, bed linens, and other materials for the housewife in making clothing or in furnishing her home. When Mr. Belk employed me, he agreed to pay me six dollars a week. But when the first Saturday night arrived, I was paid six dollars and twenty-five cents. I reasoned that the extra quarter of a dollar was in recognition of the extra long hours I had worked, although I had understood when I accepted the job that the hours would be long.

"Mr. Belk didn't lay down too many rules when he employed anyone. I remember that he just outlined certain basic principles of business, such as being courteous to customers, suggesting merchandise for them to buy, and of course he emphasized the value and importance of truthfulness, honesty, and right living."

When he first started in the Charlotte store, space was very limited, Mr. Gallant also remembers, and when the store opened the boxes of Christmas toys about the first of December, it was always a problem to find adequate space for displaying them properly. It was usually necessary to double up some of the staple merchandise carried the year around in order to provide places for the toys.

"It is remarkable how small matters become emphasized as the years pass and how certain little things remain vivid in your memory," Mr. Gallant further observes. "I can remember distinctly, although it has been forty years ago, just how good Mr. Belk was at the job of getting a lot of toys on a few small tables. I particularly remember how well he could stack up children's toy stoves and toy pianos. And at that time the stoves were made of cast iron and were pretty heavy.

"One of Mr. Belk's notions of merchandising in that day—and he still holds to it—was that everybody about a store should be able at all times to keep busy at some constructive task. I remember that he was not harsh and not a hard taskmaster, but he had little patience with indolence.

"He felt that a clerk or anyone else in the store might always to be able to find something to do, especially on rainy days when we were not busy with customers. We had a small section in the store that we called the hardware department where we sold such things as fish hooks, shears, old-time mouth harps, knives, and straight razors. On rainy days Mr. Belk would tell one or two of us to go over there and clean up the department and dust off the things on the counters. That was one of the rainy-day jobs we could always look forward to. Mr. Henry was a great fellow to have things dusted off. We were always dusting. There used to be a standing joke among the young men in the store that we'd better keep busy while Mr. Belk was around, for if he couldn't find anything else for us to do he'd send us down into the basement to dust off the coal."

Over in Monroe Dr. John Belk was doing the same kind of teaching that Henry Belk was doing in Charlotte—not by lecture but by everyday advice and example. There were the five Leggett brothers, sons of Mrs. John Belk's sister—they were from Anson County, which was next to Union County, and they were going to head one of the largest subgroups in the Belk system. John Parks was a Union County farm boy who went to the Monroe store in 1899 and also rose to leadership of the Parks-Belk subgroup in Tennessee as did his brother, C. E. Parks, in Virginia. Frank Stevens was another—he was to head the Belk-Stevens subgroup, and he was to become an even closer member of the Belk family by marrying Dr. John Belk's oldest daughter. Finally, among the future Belk leaders who grew up in the neighborhood and trained at Monroe, there was Karl G. Hudson—characteristically, one of four brothers who entered the organization. After some time in Monroe, he was sent to the new store at the neighboring town of Waxhaw, one of the very few Belk ventures that was ever discontinued. Vividly, Mr. Hudson recalls that apprenticeship:

"When I was manager of the store at Waxhaw I would go up to Monroe on the afternoon train and get back on the eleven o'clock train that night. After supper Dr. John would take time and great pains to talk to me about the principles of merchandising. Mr. Henry, when he was there, did not talk much, but he could talk if it became necessary. I remember well that in the early fall of my first year as manager at Waxhaw I had bought too heavily. I went up to Charlotte to see Mr. Henry and found him in the basement of the store. He sat down on the top of a barrel and proceeded to tell me how the Waxhaw store was broke, and he declared very emphatically that if I didn't get down to business I would be a flat failure and wouldn't amount to a jelly bean.

"It had its effect," Mr. Hudson went on. "The store was out of debt at Christmas. The day before Christmas we sold seven hundred and fifty dollars worth of merchandise, which was the biggest day we had ever had at Waxhaw. I was feeling pretty fine the next morning when I arrived at Monroe, but before I could tell Mr. Henry, who was down there that day, about the big day we had had, he beat me to it with the question: 'Karl, did you sell a thousand dollars yesterday?' He always kept us on our toes.

"Later on I got into some bad spots from time to time, but he never lectured me again and, on the contrary, was most kind and sympathetic."

Mr. Hudson feels, like many others among the associates of the merchant, that perhaps the most significant characteristic of Mr. Belk, the most distinguishing virtue, is his desire to see young men succeed.

"He is always willing to stand by a young fellow through thick and thin if he is convinced that the young man is honest, willing to work, and anxious to learn. He could never have been the success he has been had he not permitted, and required, the men associated with him in the expansion of the Belk stores to be successful and prosperous also."

Mr. Hudson had frequent opportunities to see the Belk brothers as a team, and his impression was that they were good because they balanced one another. Mr. Henry had the more decisive manner and was inclined to be quick in his judgments, but if anything important came up he always wanted his brother's advice. Dr. John was a slower, more thoughtful type—perhaps as a result of his medical training and practice. "It always seemed to me Dr. John thought out loud and always argued both sides of the question," Mr. Hudson says. "And when he had finished, Mr. Henry and he would usually know what they wanted to do."

Dr. Belk was as insistent as his brother on the absolute necessity of being courteous to everyone, regardless of the size of his pocketbook, and Mr. Hudson tells this story of an incident that reveals the practice as well as the theory:

"One day when the store was filled with people Dr. Belk saw a Negro woman come in the front door and walk all the way to the back of the store without having anyone speak to her. She had started back toward the front and was apparently about to leave. Dr. Belk made a special effort to go over and speak to her. He assured her that one of the salespeople would wait on her in a moment. His words seemed to reassure her and please her greatly.

" 'That's all right, sir,' the woman said to Dr. Belk, 'I'm in no great hurry. I just wanted to be recognized.' "

GEORGE W. DOWDY

BELK BROTHERS COMPANY, Charlotte, North Carolina

A. L. Tyler, Rocky Mount, North Carolina

Belk-Tyler, Elizabeth City, North Carolina (*credit Frisby's Studio*)

12

REGARDLESS OF THE EXPANSION OF THE BELK GROUP, THE
Charlotte store remained the chief interest of the Belk brothers
in the first decade and a half of the century. Charlotte
doubled its population in that period and had become the
largest city in North Carolina. All of the Piedmont industries
that had been getting under way in the eighties and developing in the nineties grew to adult stature. In 1905, for the first
time in history, southern cotton mills could boast that they
consumed as many bales of cotton as the northern mills, and
though the two sections were to run neck and neck for almost

another decade, there was no doubt as to where the major part of the future textile industry of the country was going to be located. In tobacco, James B. Duke's American Tobacco Company dominated the field until it was dissolved by court action in 1911, to be replaced by the present "big four" companies. By 1910 North Carolina was the leading state in total tobacco manufactures, even though cigarette smoking, whose growth was to give the state its present dominating position, was still widely regarded as an effeminate or sinful habit. And in 1904 James B. Duke began to play a further role in the development of the Piedmont by the formation of the Southern Power Company, which undertook an enormous program of hydroelectric power station construction on the rivers of North Carolina and South Carolina. Further profits from tobacco and power went into the industries that the power plants served. The Southern Railway line from Danville to Spartanburg was beginning to be called "Gold Avenue."

Charlotte was in the middle of this development, profiting not only from the factories themselves, but from the banks, insurance companies, law firms, investment houses, and real estate firms that were locating in the city to be at the center of things. In the process Charlotte was changing—from what had been really an overgrown town to something that was recognizably a modern city, with a central business section and outlying suburbs, a real skyscraper—in 1909—a public library, several colleges, and other appurtenances of a rounded urban life. With all this went new standards, new values, new desires in everything from shoes to music. No one feels the impact of such changes more quickly than the merchant, whose business life depends on his anticipation of, and quick response to, changes in what the customer wants. A good picture of what the change that Charlotte—and many another American community of that period—was undergoing meant in the way of women's taste in dress can be obtained from Miss Sarah Houston's recollection of the Belk millinery department that she presided over in the early 1900's. Miss Sarah, as she is affectionately known to the entire personnel of the Charlotte store and hundreds of others in the Belk group, only recently retired from active connection with the store, and she still retains an advisory position and a stock-holding interest. She can claim the title of being one of the pioneer career women in the South in the field of merchandising.

"Outside of Mr. Belk himself, I suppose Frank Matthews and I are about the oldest persons in point of service in the entire organization," she relates. "We both started away back there, almost too long ago now to say, and I've made many a hat, or designed it, in my day, besides the thousands I have bought on the New York market and elsewhere. Hats have been my job."

She remembers well that she began with Belk's when she was a young lady still in her teens and going to what was then called the South Graded School. One of the Belk department heads prevailed upon her to start a millinery department at the store.

"He told me to go see Mr. Belk," Miss Sarah recalls. Well, I wasn't interested. But he kept after me, and so one day I went. I was shown into Mr. Belk's office. He was sitting down before his old battered-up desk—pretty much like the one he has now except these new ones are kept nice and shiny —and he was looking over some papers. He didn't appear to notice me when I went in. But after I had sat there a minute or so he turned to face me.

" 'Brother John,' he said, 'looks after hiring the help.'

"Well, that made me right mad. I wasn't wanting any job, to start with, and his own man had asked me to come to the store, and it just made me mad. I didn't like the way he said 'hiring the help.'

"But that was just the way Mr. Belk was. Sometimes he could be mighty brusque, and he still can. But that's just his way. I soon found out that inside he's a fine and considerate man, and the inside is what counts.

"Well, I took the job, and we started the millinery department. Our store was the only store in town exclusively for millinery. Miss Ruth Anthony, who was later Mrs. Edward Dodge of Rocky Mount, was our first milliner.

"Hats! There's a lot of difference in hats now and those back in that period. Mostly in those days we made them. And sometimes it would take several days to make one hat. It depended, of course, upon how elaborate it was and what materials were used in making it. Folks nowadays, the men especially, laugh about women's hats. But they should have seen some of those creations we produced fifty years ago."

Many kinds of materials were used in making women's hats. Satin, chiffon, lace, velvet, fur, chenille and straw braids —even horsehair—went into them.

The hats of about 1903, for instance, included a favorite style composed of rows and rows of narrow lace edging. Such a hat required yards and yards of lace, sometimes as much as six bolts. Occasionally the milliner would alternate bands of maline with the lace or straw braids, and one season hats of pleated ribbon were especially popular.

The trimmings likewise were luxurious. Birds of paradise, ostrich, aigrettes, imported lace, flowers, fruits, plumes, used separately or in elaborate combinations, adorned the already elaborate hats. Long hatpins with jeweled metal heads were employed to hold the hats on stylishly coiffured heads.

"The men quarreled about women's hats then just as they do now, but I think they liked them," Miss Sarah comments. "Those hatpins, though, were pretty dangerous. I don't think I remember anybody's using elastic for keeping their hats on except Miss Sallie Davidson, Colonel E. L. Baxter Davidson's sister. Elastic was used, though, for the children. I guess Miss Sallie in that respect was the only prophet among the ladies in the change from hatpins to elastic, and it's a good thing they changed the style. It was pretty dangerous, and the men always had to watch out to keep from getting speared."

Belk's bought pattern hats in the northern markets to sell and also to be copied, Miss Sarah recalls.

"Those we sold on opening days, though, were always exclusive—never copied—and sometimes a customer would buy as many as half a dozen hats at one time," she remembers. "We didn't get new hats then as often as we do now, of course, and the ladies tried to stock up while we had what they liked."

The famous willow plume, which appeared around 1900, was one of the best-selling items offered in the Belk millinery department during the period it was in vogue. They were exquisite and quite expensive.

One of the periods most trying for the Belk's millinery department was the era of the pompadour. The women were using large rolls of hair, which they called "rats," to roll their own hair over in order to make it stand up, and this so enlarged their heads that it was difficult to get their hats on. So Miss Sarah Houston and her assistants arranged bandeaux to come down on one side of the head and frequently they sewed false curls to these bandeaux. It was necessary to keep in stock a large supply of false hair, switches, braids, and curls, along with laces, embroidery, ribbons, veils, gloves, and ruchings. A millinery store in that day was almost a museum. Certainly many of its products would deservedly find places in museums of this era.

Another problem that gave the millinery department of the Belk store in Charlotte much concern was the "rainy day hat."

"It was before the automobile had come into general use."

Miss Houston points out, "and when ladies had to be out-
doors on rainy days they were quite likely to get wet. It
was a problem to make a rainy day hat, because the ladies
insisted on fancy hats and still you couldn't use perishable
trimmings, like ostrich plumes, velvet, and other such deli-
cate materials.

"Those old-time hats were usually high on the head, with
long feathers sticking up—they just wouldn't go with these
present-day automobiles. In those days the buggies and the
automobiles—what few cars there were—were high inside and
the ladies could sit in them without ruining their hats. Nowadays you'd never be able to get into an automobile without
ruining your hat if you were wearing one of our early creations, unless you sat on the floor of the car! For a while after
they started making the cars lower the women who persisted in
wearing those hats with the high trimmings were always getting their hats damaged—plumes broken and flowers and
fruits banged up. I guess the change in the style of hats followed somewhat as a result of the change in the style of
automobiles."

Miss Sarah still remembers the thrill she had when one
of her hats was the subject of a lavishly commendatory style
article in a Paris newspaper.

"I made it for Celeste Wilder, later Mrs. Kenneth Blake of
New York. The hat was made entirely of pink rose petals.
She went to Paris to study music and languages and the hat
attracted so much attention that it was given a write-up in one
of the Paris papers. Later she had a life-size portrait done
of herself wearing this hat. It was a beauty, if I do say so."

Although movies were still something of a curiosity, and
neither the movie star nor the picture magazine had been
thought of, styles were beginning to be highly responsive to
such phenomena as current best-selling novels and popular
plays. The tempo of American life was speeding up.

"I remember very distinctly—and who of my generation doesn't?—the Merry Widow hat that was all the rage after the opera by that name became popular. And the Eugenie, after the life story of the empress was published. Just as, in recent times, 'Gone With The Wind' had a noticeable effect upon the style in hats."

Miss Sarah recalls vividly the excitement of the semi-annual trips north when the buyers from the various Belk stores, usually as a group, went to New York and Baltimore to see the new fashions. Mr. Henry was usually with them.

"He was a good buyer, too. He knew materials and he knew how to locate bargains. I remember he used to buy a lot of stock from Charles Broadway Rouse. Broadway, I always understood, was his real name. Anyway, he was a great merchant in those days and Mr. Belk did a lot of trading with him. He would pay Mr. Rouse for a bill of merchandise and then Mr. Rouse would credit him with another bill. When he paid for the bill that had been credited, the New York man would credit him with another order. I think that's the way they worked it back then when the stores were getting started.

"But there's one thing you can say about Mr. Belk in connection with my department—he left that to me. He kept his finger in everything that went on at the store and the other stores as they got started, and he knew what business we were doing and all that, of course, but he certainly didn't fool around with women's hats.

"In fact, he didn't even come into the millinery department very often. Some mornings he'd peep in the front door, but if there were several women in there trying on hats he'd very likely back out quickly and go on down to his store just below us. Some folks said he was bashful and afraid of the ladies. I don't know about that. But I know he didn't undertake to monkey with women's hats. He left the millinery department pretty much to me and as long as we got along all right he didn't pay us any great attention."

All the new needs of the people of Charlotte made themselves felt at Belk Brothers, and by 1908 the need for more space at the store was crucial. They had already expanded once by leasing an adjoining building. Their location was a good one, but it was no longer possible to adopt to their requirements such a makeshift arrangement. So they bought a larger tract of adjacent property, and built what was in effect a new five-story store, using the two old stores as annexes.

Of this new store a newspaper article declared years later: "It was the first real department store, certainly in Charlotte, probably in the Carolinas. . . . For almost ten years, Belk Brothers was the single department store in the city. Its influence was far reaching. Even in the dark ages when the roads of Carolina were not even a promise of the present paved highways, farmers brought their families to Belks. Many of them loaded up the old farm wagon with the entire family and brought them in. Charlotte was their stopping place, Belks their destination." The Belks had shown that they could anticipate the new needs of the people of Charlotte.

In the days before high income taxes, prosperity in Charlotte and in the other towns having Belk stores gave the brothers a chance to do what they failed to accomplish in the dark days in Monroe. There were profits over and above the needs of the stores for investment. Local investment had a wider meaning in Charlotte than it had in Monroe but the principle was the same, and both company surplus and their own money went into North Carolina and southern enterprises. Perhaps Scotch-Irish shrewdness dictated that they put their money where they could watch it closely. And certainly a merchant's common sense would lead him to invest in such a way as to produce more payrolls and acquire more customers. But beyond that it was their feeling for their home region—the same feeling that made them staff their stores with Union County and other home boys—that kept their investments largely in their home community. Their interests were too highly diversified—cotton mills, garment factories, hotels and office buildings, farm implement manufacturing companies, telephone companies, banks, flour mills—but in nearly every case they represented an investment in a local future.

In the two years immediately preceding America's entry into the First World War, the Belk group made its most significant expansion in any two-year period up to that time. The whole group was doing a business of around two million dollars a year by this time, and it could afford now to push out rapidly. Five new stores were added—in Greenville, South Carolina, and in Rockingham, Kannapolis, Winston-Salem, Raleigh, and Wilmington in North Carolina. Greenville and Kannapolis fell within the pattern set by earlier expansions— they were thriving textile towns not too far from Charlotte on the Southern Railway; and Rockingham was a small town of a type familiar to the Belks from childhood, the county seat of a cotton county. But Winston-Salem, Raleigh, and Wilmington were three of the state's most important cities, all jealous in one way or another of Charlotte's new preeminence as the state's first city. Raleigh was the capital, and Wilmington for generations had been the state's seaport and leading city—until Charlotte overtook it. Both were accustomed to smile a bit—and occasionally to sneer—at the hustlers in the west. Even more important from the practical point of view, both were beyond the radius of a hundred miles from Charlotte, within which it was easy for the Belks to get around. It was important to have the right men for the jobs of managing the stores in these cities.

The right men were waiting for the opportunity, trained under the careful tutelage of the brothers in Monroe and

Charlotte. Frank Stevens, the Union County boy who had become manager of the Monroe store and married Dr. John Belk's daughter Nealie in 1912, was the choice for the Belk-Stevens store in Winston-Salem. Karl G. Hudson, whose impressions of the Belks were gained in a long apprenticeship in the organization and who was thoroughly familiar with their operational methods and principles, was ready to take charge of the Hudson-Belk store in Raleigh. Characteristically, he took with him as associates two of his brothers, J. G. Hudson and W. J. Hudson, and the brothers were to develop an important subgroup of stores later. And still another Waxhaw boy trained in the Belk stores—Jim Williams—was chosen for the Wilmington store managership.

Even before America entered the war, the success of the new stores seemed firmly established; the Belk group was now truly a system extending through the Carolinas.

13

B<small>UT THERE WAS ONE EVENT IN THE LIFE OF HENRY BELK</small> that took his attention—perhaps for the first time in his business life—completely away from the affairs of the Belk store.

In the spring of 1915 the Charlotte *News* on its society page one day reported, with the effusiveness common to society pages of all times and places, the following:

"The meeting of the Chelidon Book Club with Mrs. Edward C. Dwelle at their pretty home on North College Street this afternoon had a meaning all its own for the members and

state society at large, for at this meeting Mrs. Dwelle announced the engagement and approaching marriage of Miss
Mary Lenora Irwin and Mr. William Henry Belk, the marriage to take place early in June."

The announcement, the society editor went on to reveal,
"came as a delightful and happy surprise—not that the social
ear had failed in its quickness and had not caught the interesting whisper the spring days had brought, but the very
definiteness of the announcement today was the surprise."

The article continues with an account of how Fay Ross
Dwelle, the little daughter of the hostess, "wearing white lace
over silk, her ribbons pink, entered bearing a large silver tray
on which were a number of tiny envelopes tied with pink
ribbon," inside of which were the words:

Mary Lenora Irwin
William Henry Belk
June, 1915

"Miss Irwin was strikingly handsome in an exquisite gown
of pale green silk net over taffeta, with corsage, from her
fiancé, of pink roses and lilies of the valley. . . .

"Miss Irwin is a daughter of Dr. and Mrs. John R. Irwin,
the former one of Charlotte's most prominent physicians and
leading citizens. Educated at Queen's College [Presbyterian
College] and a graduate thereof, Miss Irwin at once entered
society and became one of the most popular young women
in her set.

"Possessing a mind of unusual alertness, reading and loving the best in literature, fond of travel and having an ap-
preciative sense of the beauties of book and country, Miss
Irwin is easily one of the most charming girls in the city.

"Miss Irwin is a descendant of John McKnitt Alexander of
Mecklenburg Declaration fame. She is a member of Mecklenburg Chapter, D.A.R., a member of Stonewall Jackson

U.D.C., and of The Colonial Dames and the Chelidon Book Club."

And of her fiancé the society reporter wrote:

"Mr. Belk is president and manager of the great group of department stores, known throughout the state as Belk Bros., he and his brother, Dr. John Belk, of Monroe, constituting the firm, the main store being the big department store on East Trade Street. A native of Union County, Mr. Belk has resided in Charlotte for a number of years and is today rated as one of the leading men of affairs not only in Charlotte but the state. . . . He has a genius for business and this genius has given to Charlotte one of its richest mercantile assets—Belk Bros. Department Store. Mr. Belk is not only esteemed for his business ability, but for his personal worth. A man of highest integrity, foremost in church and state in the matter of civic or religious betterment, he wields an influence at once flattering and powerful. Few men in this section stand higher in the public regard than Mr. Henry Belk, and the news of the happiness that is to come into his life, thereby completing the one chapter missing, will be heard with intense interest throughout the Carolinas."

But this eloquence of the society columns was not employed by the average Charlottean who for years had been wondering why Henry Belk did not get married. For a long time they had been describing him simply as "a mighty good catch for some lucky girl."

He had indeed been slow in getting around to the business of writing this "one chapter missing" in his very busy life. His friends had virtually assigned him to the single blessedness that his contemporary in Boston, Edward A. Filene, would continue in to the end of his days.

But Henry Belk had always thought of himself as a family man. It was a part of the religion that he had learned from his mother, and that grew stronger in him every year. Every week it was renewed on his Sunday trips down to Monroe to go to church with her. She was now approaching eighty, revered by all the community, and in the strength and simplicity of her faith she must have wished that her older son, who over the years had done so much for the family would now have a family of his own.

And in his brother John's family there would also have been a prompting to Henry Belk. Brother John had chosen to remain in Monroe and raise a family. Henry had had the more strenuous role—the day-to-day decisions on buying, the travelling to New York, the faster tempo of the Charlotte store. John's special contribution to the partnership was the quiet wisdom he brought to the big problems and his extraordinary ability as a teacher of the Waxhaw boys who were carrying the Belk way of doing business across the Carolinas. John had built himself a big home and raised a family—seven daughters, the oldest of whom had already married Frank Stevens and the youngest of whom was now seven. Henry Belk had watched them all growing up. And he had been touched by Brother John's wish to have a son that he might name for Henry. When the sixth child was born—a girl—he threw convention to the wind and named her for his brother. It was not hard, when the next and last was also a girl, to name her John.

All of this must have had its effect, perhaps unrecognized by him, on Henry Belk. For years all the emotional side of his life had been directed toward his business. As he neared and then passed fifty, he must have felt that if he was to have a life of his own, he must make a decision soon. Business life had not worn him down—pictures of him reveal a sturdy tall man without a line in his face or a touch of gray in his hair. His countenance was one that would have been somewhat stern and commanding had it not been for a crinkle at the corners of his eyes and a genial mobility in his mouth.

Henry Belk's own version of his romance has the simplicity characteristic of the man:

"I was a full generation late in getting married," he said many years later. "I should have been my own children's grandfather. A lot of people have asked me why I was so slow in getting married. Some of them figured I was just too bashful to do any courting along about the usual time young people do their courting."

"Well, I reckon maybe I was a little bashful around the girls. But that really wasn't the reason. I was just too busy working. I worked night and day back in those years, trying to get my business established. I worked mighty long hours. There wasn't much time left for courting if I'd had a mind to. When the other young men were hiring fancy rigs at the livery stable and taking the girls out for rides, I was usually busy at the store, checking up the stock and getting it laid out for the next day's business. And Sundays I generally spent with my mother.

"Dr. Irwin's family lived down on North Tryon Street across the street from the Episcopal Church, and I had known them a good while. But I didn't get interested in Mary until the summer I went on a pleasure trip out through the West. Mary was on the trip, and so were several other Charlotte young ladies.

"Well, there was an old fellow on the train; he was a widower. He was trying to catch himself another wife and he took a great liking to Mary. One day he came to me and told me about her.

" 'I want you to help me out with her,' he said.

"I told him, sort of joking then, of course, that I might help him out, but I wasn't sure.

" 'I might be interested myself,' I told him.

"Well, the upshot of it was that I did help him out. Yes, sir, I helped him clean out with Mary. But he didn't have a chance anyway, I'm sure. And anyhow, he ought not to have acted like Miles Standish did with John Alden. In courting, like in a lot of other things, it's a pretty good idea for a man to speak for himself."

He was one week past his fifty-third birthday when on Wednesday, June 9, 1915, with his brother John standing beside him as best man, in the parlor of the Irwin home on North Tryon Street, he renounced his bachelorhood.

BELK-McKNIGHT COMPANY, Griffin, Georgia
BELK-HUDSON COMPANY, Spartanburg, South Carolina

BELK-JONES COMPANY, Texarkana, Arkansas

BELK-HUDSON COMPANY, Talladega, Alabama

V

MERCHANT OF THE SOUTH

14

DURING THE COURSE OF THE FIRST WORLD WAR THERE
was practically no expansion in the Belk stores. A store in
Albemarle, North Carolina, which was opened a few months
after America's entry into the war, was the only new store
opened in 1917 and 1918. Compared with what was to come
in the Second World War, there were no controls on American business and industry. On the home front the war was
fought with voluntary "wheatless days" and "meatless days"
and with Boy Scouts selling Liberty Bonds. The South was
dotted with training camps, and all along the railroads lead-

ing north, patriotic women set up canteens to give doughnuts and hot coffee to the soldiers moving toward ports for embarkation to Europe. All in all, the young industrial giant of America was to produce guns and butter too, in greater abundance than ever before.

Nevertheless, while the war lasted, the Belks found themselves fully occupied in the expanding business of the existing stores. During the war period and for two years after, everything went up—farm prices, wages, the cost of living. Southern farmers had never seen anything like it—thirty-five and forty cents a pound for cotton, fifty cents a pound for tobacco. They could think about getting Ford cars for their farms and ready-made clothes for their women folk. The industrial workers too, spurred on by Henry Ford's revolutionary policy of paying the unprecedented sum of five dollars a day to his workers, were thinking in new terms. All through 1919 and 1920, the great strikes in coal and steel and other industries expressed the workers' determination to keep abreast of the times. The salaried people and the white-collar workers—and the war had brought many women into this group—were feeling the pinch of high prices; their incomes had not kept up with the soaring cost of living.

The expansion of the Belk stores in the immediate postwar period was typical of the increased tempo of the times. In 1919 and 1920, twelve new stores were added to the seventeen already established; it was far and away the most rapid expansion the Belk organization had made thus far. Most of the stores were in North Carolina, but four new ones were in South Carolina, and the new one in Danville, Virginia, marked the first step outside the Carolinas. Most of the new stores were in the Piedmont area, and with Belk stores in Danville, in High Point and Durham, North Carolina, and in Spartanburg, South Carolina, there were now

Belk stores in practically every important city in the industrial area of the Piedmont.

The period was notable in the Belk history because it saw the beginning of three of the most important of the subgroups in the Belk family of stores. The Belk-Leggett stores in Danville and Durham were headed by the Leggett brothers, who were kinsmen of the Belks, and they were to expand into numerous other cities in Virginia and North Carolina. The Gallant-Belk store in Anderson, South Carolina, headed by the W. E. Gallant who had been learning merchandising in the Charlotte store since 1906, was to be the parent store of the large Gallant-Belk sub-group. Likewise the Belk-Tyler store in Rocky Mount, headed by Arthur L. Tyler, one of the very few important Belk leaders who did not get his primary training in a Belk store, was to be the hub of the very successful Belk-Tyler sub-group in eastern North Carolina.

But in 1920 the price structure upon which the postwar boom had been built collapsed, and the whole country faced a reckoning for the wartime inflation. Almost overnight cotton and tobacco prices were cut in half and continued to go down. The American farmer was not destined to share the prosperity that was to come later in the twenties. For the industrial worker, breadline succeeded picket lines as factories closed and businesses failed. Many a merchant who had bought in a frenzy whatever he could get at the high prices of 1919 and 1920 found himself with an inventory that was a millstone around his neck.

The violent readjustment was a testing time for a business that had just expanded as rapidly as the Belk stores had. They passed the test. Not a single Belk store had to close its doors. It was probably in the long run a great advantage to Henry Belk and his brother that they had started out in business for themselves during one of the toughest periods in

American business life. It made them distrustful of the quick rises and the sudden good times. Six months before the price break came at the end of 1920, the Belks had become suspicious. They had advised the store managers to slow up on buying and to cut down their inventories by reducing prices. Many of their competitors thought they were fools to mark their goods down while high prices still prevailed. But when the general break came, the Belk inventories generally were clean, and they could begin buying at the lower prices that prevailed.

And again the cash basis of operating showed its advantages. There were few creditors to placate, no customers to dun. The Belk position was sound—sound enough, in fact, to make it possible for them to help out other enterprises that were in trouble.

Chief among these were the cotton mills. The South was now clearly in the lead in textiles, and North Carolina was the leading state in the country in that industry. But the cotton textile industry as a whole was not in good condition—it was not well organized as an industry, it had over expanded in the war period, and it was beginning to get severe competition from other fabrics. The South suffered particularly because its leading position was based on production of the coarser fabrics now in less demand. As merchants, the Belks could see the new demands of the public before the manufacturers themselves could; and during this particular crisis, as well as later, they put their money into mills to enable them to purchase equipment for producing finer fabrics.

The depression of 1921 was sharp, but it did not last long. By 1923 the country was entering the great boom. Many books have been written about the achievements and the follies of that period. A merchant could have any of a number of opinions on such topics of that time as the lost generation, the emancipated woman, prohibition, the Harding scandals, the Chicago racketeers, the radio, or Wall Street speculation —or innumerable others. But as a sober businessman, trying to sense and satisfy the public's desires, he would be concerned chiefly with two major developments. First, there was the fact that American industry and technical skill, matured by the war, could now produce a bewildering variety of material goods of all sorts, and the boom put enough money in the hands of the average American to allow him to pick and choose among the good things offered. The second problem that the merchant faced was the fact that in this period the chain stores began to push the independent merchant to the wall.

In the twenties, an America that had clothed itself largely in the simpler kinds of cottons and woolens turned to a bewildering variety of fabrics, some of them developed from older fabrics, some, like silk, old fabrics now within the range of average pocketbooks, and some, like rayon, new. An America that largely made its own clothes at home turned toward the ready-made dress from the merchant's rack. The American kitchen, as advertised in that period, would hardly have been recognizable as a kitchen to the customer's grandmother. A billion-dollar industry in cosmetics grew up in a decade, with its service stations, the beauty parlors, in every village. The American pocketbook could afford hundreds of new gadgets for the house, and hundreds of new adornments for its owners.

It was a vast opportunity for department stores such as the Belks were running, but an opportunity that brought its perils with it. With such a profusion you could make a lot more mistakes in buying. More and more the buyer had to be an expert in materials with a genius for guessing which way the public's fancy would jump.

If you approach Mr. Belk today with a compliment about his success or great shrewdness as a merchant, he will very quickly discount it.

"In fact—" Mr. Belk will pause, look you in the eye, and confide, in his characteristic method of understatement—"in fact, anybody could have done what I have done. I'm not so smart. I've made a lot of mistakes. I've lost money; I haven't always been on the black side in every trade. But I have always been willing to work hard, and I have always tried to please my customers. Any young man of ordinary talents who is willing to work hard and for long hours and keep his eyes open and his mind on his business can do well—as well as I have done in the store business, I'd say."

Naturally, Henry Belk would not have been infallible in a period such as the twenties. Occasionally his vision into the future was none too clear—like other merchants of that time, he saw profits that did not materialize. One of the more famous mirages has come to be known by Belk managers everywhere as the case of the high-topped shoes.

"It was about the end of the First World War," a manager recently recalled. "The high-topped women's shoes, both in the button and lace models, had been popular. But about the time that Mr. Henry had an opportunity to buy up a tremendous stock of them at an excellent price, the market for them began to slow up—after the war women stopped wearing them at all and took to low shoes. Pretty soon we were stuck with those high-topped shoes.

"Well, those of us who already had them got rid of them sooner or later. Most of us marked them so low they just had to move. If they didn't move then we marked them down some more. But Mr. Henry wouldn't give up. I guess it became a matter of principle with him. It got to be a test of a new manager's ability—whether he could get rid of those high-topped shoes. When a new store was opened, Mr. Henry, as a matter of inventory selection, would suggest to the new manager that he take some of those 'fine high-button shoes.' The smart ones took some of the shoes and got rid of them somehow. I understand a lot of them ended up as gifts to mountain missions. Anyway, that was one case in which Mr. Henry figured wrong. But he didn't often bite off more than he could chew. He's generally a mighty shrewd buyer."

The faster tempo of fashion changes in the twenties did produce one important development in the Belks' operations. New York City had become practically the exclusive wholesale center for most department store lines, displacing such former competitors as Philadelphia and Baltimore. Belk buyers from the various stores still made trips to New York, usually, as in the past, in a group and after a meeting with Mr. Henry in Charlotte. But more frequent trips were now necessary, if the stores were to keep up with the times. The Charlotte store was still much the biggest of the group, and for some years it had had a representative in New York, Alfred Fantl, for the New York and foreign markets. By 1924 the pressure was too great, and the Charlotte store set up a permanent buying office in New York under the direction of Miss Emma Weiss, now Mrs. Sam Brown. It was a natural development that the New York office of the Charlotte store would serve the needs of the other stores in the intervals between buying trips, advise them on new trends, and in general, make itself useful to the entire family of stores. The New York office was to increase in size each year.

Chain stores had been growing in the United States since before 1900, but in the twenties they spread like wildfire. It has been estimated that in the period from 1919 to 1927, the five-and-ten chains increased their business by 160 per cent, the drug chains by 125 per cent, and the food chains by nearly 300 per cent. And while no great national chain in the department store field emerged, in many states and regions chain department stores did come into existence. And the five-and-ten stores, in particular, forgot all about the price limitations which their signs proclaimed, added more expensive lines, and became in effect low-price department stores organized in national chains.

It was a logical development of the desire for bigness that was the ideal of most American business men. If you were a merchant and had made some money in your store, you set up another and put a manager in. Then another and another, until you had spread across your state, across your region, across the whole country. It was your store, and the managers were your employees. You could get the advantage of buying in large quantities, of buying direct from the manufacturer, or even owning your own manufacturing plants. As for moving the goods, you could get the most expert advice in advertising, in merchandising, in promotion, and you could tell the managers exactly how to go about it—what lines to push, what prices to sell at, how to manage their units.

The chain-store idea worked—that is, it frequently made money in a big way. But it had its disadvantages, though they were less apparent in the twenties than they are now. In the first place, the local manager had no stake in the community in which he was working—while his sales record was carefully watched from on high, and he would be fired or advanced on what it showed, he was not really a part of his town but a transient who might be transferred at any moment to another unit, or let out altogether. And he had no great stake in his company either—unless he could be one of the lucky few who would be picked for a position in the main office. Nor would the community treat him as a member—he was working for a big corporation that was taking all the profits out of the community. Resentment would flare up from time to time in small communities where a local merchant, whose father and grandfather perhaps had run his store before him, had been forced out of business because he could not meet chain competition. Another difficulty was that all the high-priced experts at the main office were unable to help the manager in solving problems that were purely local, and he did not have the freedom to tackle these problems with his own solutions. All the main office could do was to put on more pressure for sales. The chain store worked, but at a cost—it did not develop good men at the local level. In fact, it tended to wear them out.

In 1922, when the chain-store idea was taking hold in a big way, the Belk organization comprised thirty-one stores scattered over the Carolinas, and one store in Virginia; in all there were about two thousand people working in the stores, and the volume of business was in the neighborhood of six million dollars a year. Given the times, the growing problem of size, the increasing complexity of buying, the idea of turning the group into a chain must have occurred to the Belks.

In fact, the idea was presented later, shortly after the Belks employed E. A. Anderson in 1927.

Mr. Anderson, now controller of the Belk stores system, with a walnut panelled office in the new Belk Buying Service building in Charlotte, was young and ambitious and eager to be of maximum service to the organization.

He began looking over the Belk books and checking facts and figures around the Belk establishment, and after a while he had an idea. He worked all his spare moments at the office to perfect his plan; he took the figures home with him at nights, and with sharpened pencils and reams of paper he worked over it until he was satisfied that it could not be improved upon.

Then he took it to Mr. Belk.

"I had worked hard on it," he said almost a quarter of a century later. "I had sat up late at nights poring over figures, working out the plan to the smallest detail. I felt mighty good that morning I took it to Mr. Henry. I just knew I had worked out a master scheme that would do wonders for the Belk business.

"I suppose I was grinning when I handed Mr. Belk the papers. I could hardly wait to hear what he would say.

"Well, he took the papers, glanced at them.

" 'What's this?' he asked.

" 'Mr. Belk,' I said, 'I've been working on this during my spare time here at the office and at nights at home. This—' I pointed to the papers in his hand—'is a plan for the organization of all the Belk stores under one corporate structure to provide for joint operation of the stores under one—'

" 'What? What are you saying?' he interrupted.

"I started over to explain that in my spare time, without any extra pay, I had devised a plan for the organization of the Belk stores as one corporation, as a single entity directed from a central headquarters.

" 'Here, take these papers!' he almost yelled at me as he thrust them back in my hand. 'Take 'em and tear 'em up quick! I don't want to look at 'em. I don't want to know anything about 'em. Don't even think of such a thing again! Don't ever mention it!'

"That was the end of the Belk chain-store system. It died before it was born. And it was the proper thing that it should die before it could be started. Mr. Belk had the right idea. Time has abundantly demonstrated the wisdom of not having a Belk chain-store system. The great success of the Belk family of stores, the way I see it, can be attributed to the fact that it is not a chain-store system but instead is simply a growing family of stores, each independent of the others, but all working together in a fraternal sense to help the others.

"Mr. Belk foresaw this years ago. That is why he is a great merchant. He can see far into the future. If there's anybody who properly can be called long-headed, it's Mr. Belk."

Henry Belk is usually a gentle and quiet-spoken man, and his explosive violence on this occasion is evidence of the strength of his feelings. He did not want to be a dictator.

While he and his brother wanted to sell as much merchandise as they could, they did not worship bigness for bigness' sake. More than that, they were still rooted in the community that they grew up in, and they knew what it meant for a man to have a stake in his community. The Belk stores were to be run so that the head of an individual store could put down roots, have a real sense of ownership in the enterprise he headed, and a direct profit from the success of his effort. The Union County boys that they had trained to be merchants would have the same chance that they had. If the Belks also had the shrewd suspicion that in the long run their system would produce more profits than a chain-store organization, their attitude was no more contradictory than the belief that democracy is good in itself, and also works better than dictatorship.

Nevertheless, there was the problem of size. The Belk group was not doing big business by the standards of the twenties or by the standards it was to achieve later. But thirty-one stores were still a good number, particularly if you were not going to sit in Charlotte and give orders, but try to supply leadership, give good advice tailored to local situations, and in general help the men on the spot to achieve their own success.

The kind of leadership that is needed to achieve those ends can hardly be explained, but there are stories about the Belks that illustrate how they operated. It is not surprising, for instance, that a Presbyterian of Henry Belk's conviction would use a parable or a fable in a business situation. Karl Hudson tells a story to illustrate it.

"I remember back in the 1920's when we were having a rather hard time of it following World War I. We were still a rather small group of stores in those days, certainly as compared with the present time. On this particular occasion we were having a meeting of the managers of all the stores.

We were discussing the fact that we had bought too many goods. We were much concerned about the situation, too. Finally Mr. Henry, who hadn't had much to say, spoke up:

" 'You fellows all remind me of an old bullfrog I heard about once. He was sitting out beside the pool hollering "Belly-deep, belly-deep," when an ox came up and said, "Mr. Frog, you think you are mighty big, don't you?" The frog said, "I am not as big as you are, Mr. Ox, but I can be; just watch me!" Then the old frog began to blow himself up, and he got larger and larger; and then the first thing he knew all of a sudden he busted all to pieces.'

"That's the way Mr. Henry had of telling us that we were all trying to be big too fast."

Another of Karl Hudson's stories shows how the Belks could use silence alone as a persuading device.

"Jim Williams of Wilmington once told me how on one occasion he wanted to do a certain thing and Dr. Belk invited him to come up to Monroe to meet with him and Mr. Henry. Jim said he went up from Wilmington and Mr. Henry came down from Charlotte. They had supper together and after supper Dr. Belk kept the conversation going on about other things until the time came for the train to leave for Charlotte and Mr. Henry had left without their having got around to the subject that Jim had come all the way from Wilmington to discuss with them. Jim told me that he always felt that it was the Belks' way of saying no to him."

But the chief method was that of giving a man they trusted the right to make his own mistakes, and learn thereby. Again Karl Hudson tells the story, this one on himself.

"When we were planning a new store here in Raleigh, I wrote Mr. Henry about a building that was for sale in Raleigh. A short time later he came into the store and said he had looked over the building in question but did not think well of the idea of buying it.

" 'However,' he added, 'this vacant lot next door to you would be a fine buy if it could be bought for a reasonable price.' He said he had just stepped the lot off and that it had a frontage of more than a hundred feet. He told me that if the lot could be bought for $75,000 it would be a fine deal. Several days later I called him and reported that I had been able to get the owners down to $125,000 and that I would like very much to buy it.

" 'Are you sure that it is what you want to do?' he asked me.

"I told him I was sure it would be a good proposition.

" 'Well, then,' he said, 'you had better go ahead and buy it.'

"So we bought it and began making plans for our new store. Mr. Henry suggested that we have four floors and a basement. But I argued that three floors and a basement would be all we would ever need. Five years after we moved into the building we realized that we did need that extra floor. In talking with Mr. Henry one day I spoke of my mistake and his having been right in suggesting four floors. But he didn't offer any 'I told you so' remarks.

" 'Karl,' he said, 'You were undertaking a big thing and you did what you thought was best. It was better to do what you knew you could do and not get over your head.' "

15

T HERE IS NO DOUBT THAT HENRY BELK ENJOYED THE JOB he had set himself of giving democratic guidance to a grow-ing family of stores. There were, of course, regular times when store executives came to Charlotte. Every year there were the directors' meetings—a separate meeting for each individual store—usually held in the Charlotte office, unless state laws where the store was located required otherwise. Since most of the managers were stockholders and directors of their own stores, there was nothing perfunctory about these meetings—they were business conferences between the parties

D. J. Bostian, Charlotte, North Carolina

Sarah Houston, Charlotte, North Carolina

P. P. SCARBORO, Wadesboro, North Carolina

W. A. BENTON, Hamlet, North Carolina

directly concerned with the welfare of each store. And usually the regular buying trips north were preceded by meetings of the buyers in the Charlotte stores to discuss changes in styles and fashions, inventory problems, and general business conditions. But that was the smallest part of the job. Henry Belk, with his instinct for "trading and trafficking," was always running across big bargains—merchandise that he could get at a good price if he took a huge quantity, goods from liquidation sales, direct purchases from manufacturers. Distributing such goods he had purchased was not a matter of orders to the various stores to take certain quantities but of more "trading and trafficking" with the individual managers. He had trained them to be independent in their judgments, and he was willing to abide by their decisions. Finally, there were local problems in each of the stores, and the managers were always eager to get the advice of a man whose shrewdness was seasoned with fifty years' experience as a merchant in the South.

It meant a lot of travelling for Henry Belk—for he, rather than his brother, did most of this work. And the trips were getting to be longer, for in the twenties the Belk stores were pushing out farther and farther from the hub at Charlotte. By the end of the period there were stores as far north as Lynchburg, Virginia; as far south as Athens, Georgia; as far west as Kingsport, Tennessee. It was not like the days when every store was within a two or three-hour train trip. He would have noticed, in these trips, how the automobile and the hardsurfaced road were revolutionizing the South. It was particularly noticeable in North Carolina, because that state in the early twenties had taken a deep breath and mortgaged its future with a fifty million dollar bond issue to build in a hurry a new system of highways and schools. North Carolina's speculation was successful—the roads brought new life to towns that had been languishing on branch lines of railroads. More important still from a merchant's point of view, the roads added square miles to the area from which a store could attract its customers. As other southern states put through road-building programs, the horizons lifted for a great expansion in the smaller towns of the South. Before the war Belk expansion had been largely determined by railroad development—chiefly the Southern Railway System in the Carolina Piedmont. From now on the highway network would be equally important. The Belk expansion in the future was to put special emphasis on the smaller towns—towns like Monroe that the Belks knew so well—that were being given new vigor by the automobile and the truck.

But it is safe to say that during the twenties Henry Belk got more enjoyment out of the development of Charlotte than out of any expansion of the Belk family into new territory. The Charlotte store was his headquarters, and it was the store in which he had personal command. There he could slip out of his office and get out on the floor himself— as he continued to do—greeting a customer, talking up a bargain, or helping one of the salespersons. It was where he felt the real fulfillment of his childhood ambition.

Charlotte was still the biggest city served by a Belk store. It was now around seventy-five thousand in population—over twice the number of people who were there when the Belks had astounded the community with their big addition to the store in 1908. That addition had been expected to serve for an indefinite future. But less than twenty years later it was already much too cramping. Again the Belks chose, not a completely new store, but a further addition. The addition brought the total store area to 120,000 square feet—they had started in Charlotte with a store area of 2,250 square feet. In the process of building the addition the two older stores were remodelled and absorbed in the new, so that what emerged was a new store, with all the display devices and merchandising gadgets that the experts were developing in the twenties. In addition to the space it provided for a fully departmented retail store, the new store provided an entire fifth floor for a huge wholesale sample room, where Henry Belk's bargains could be examined by the buyers of the other stores in the Belk family.

On opening day, more than twenty-five thousand people stormed the doors, from Charlotte itself and from the country-side, and twelve thousand souvenirs were given away. It was a strenuous but exciting day for the nearly four hundred people who staffed the store. For the Belk brothers and for the other old-timers—Frank Matthews, the general manager, his brother W. M. Matthews, the treasurer, Miss Sarah Houston, the manager and buyer for the second floor—it was a day that brought back vivid memories of a quarter of a century and more of merchandising.

As the great boom of the twenties headed toward its climax, Henry Belk, if he had been a vain man, could have congratulated himself on having done well for himself—not as well, perhaps, as some of the spectacular successes whose names were splashed in the headlines, but well enough. The total Belk business, which had been around six million dollars a year in 1922, was now more than twelve million annually. To the thirty-one stores that had existed in 1922, seventeen had been added—in the Carolinas, in Virginia, in Georgia, in Tennessee.

And the growth had been solid. Actually, he had been conservative, as far as the number of new stores added to the family was concerned. There were chains that could show many times more new units than the number of new stores in the Belk group. But the Belk system of store relationships had worked—the managers and co-owners had responded to the challenge of responsibility and a share of the profits of their own endeavor and had made the most of the individual stores. The Belk training had helped—unfailing courtesy, cash prices that would meet all competition, no questions asked about the return of goods. And of course the substantial growth of nearly all the communities in which Belk stores were located had made for a natural increase in the business of a well-run store. Places like Durham and Winston-Salem and Greensboro and Spartanburg were now cities in a class with Charlotte itself, and the smaller cities and towns aided by the automobile had vastly increased their total trading areas. The Belk family had grown with the growth of the region it lived in.

And it had been done without resorting to any of the kinds of experts that were the idols of that period. He and his brother had not had to call in a New York lawyer or banker or investment broker or advertising expert. They had resisted the lure of the chain-store system, and also that other popular device for exercising control without responsibility —the device of the holding company. They had done their financing on their own or with the aid of the Charlotte banks; and the individual stores were encouraged to use the banks of their own localities for commercial loans. Although they had begun, in the late twenties, to use some advertising in national magazines, they had not fallen under the spell of that prima donna of the twenties, the New York advertising agency. Most of the advertising of the Belk family of stores had been local advertising, of course, and thus the responsibility of the individual store manager. Some stores had used the radio, but for the most part the stores had followed the Belk philosophy of making the satisfied customer the advertiser of the stores.

As for their personal accumulations—and they were considerable in this period—neither of the Belks responded to the siren call of the big bull market. Their investments went where they had gone before—into the textile mills, utilities, banks, office buildings, and other manufacturing enterprises of their region. All of this was a part of the Belk way of doing business.

The depression was just ahead, but before it arrived, Henry Belk suffered a loss that was incomparably harder to bear than any of the business troubles of the future.

On March 21, 1928, the year before the great crash, his brother died. For Henry Belk it was a great tragedy; the two men since their earliest childhood days had been devoted to each other, and through their adult years each had leaned heavily upon the other. They had been a great team—in their family relationships, their business ventures, their philanthropies. From now on Henry Belk would be on his own.

Dr. Belk died on the day his father would have been ninety-five years old. Had he lived until July 12, he would have been sixty-three. His mother then was ninety-two, and her long life had already been notched with great sorrow, though the latter years had been more serene than the earlier ones. But faith and work had continued to sustain her, and the love of her children.

The death of Dr. Belk ended in fact though not in name the "partnership" of Belk Brothers Company, and hereafter the responsibility of directing the business would fall alone upon Henry Belk, who forty years before had established it.

Dr. Belk's will, admitted for probate by the clerk of the court in Monroe, gave official and final evidence to the respect and devotion he held for his older brother.

"I hereby appoint my brother, W. H. Belk, of Charlotte, the executor of this my last will and testament, giving him all the powers and authorities herein expressed, and upon his death, if my estate has not yet been settled, I nominate and appoint my daughter, Mabel Belk, and my son-in-law, A. F. Stevens, to qualify as executors and wind up my estate, giving to him the same powers herein conferred upon my executor, W. H. Belk, but they shall have nothing to do with said estate during the lifetime of my brother, W. H. Belk, and shall only take charge of same as executors upon his death."

At another place in the will Dr. Belk provided that, "If any dispute arises as to the authority of my executor herein named, or his successors, or if any dispute or misunderstanding should arise as to the construction of any paragraph or any word or phrase in this my last will and testament, the construction placed hereon by my brother, W. H. Belk, is hereby declared to be binding upon the devisees and legatees herein named. I desire this for two reasons. First, I have the utmost confidence in his ability and integrity, and second, I desire no litigation over my estate."

The property was left to the seven daughters. Mrs. Belk had died ten years before.

Dr. Belk specified that the partnership in the Monroe store should be continued and should be managed by W. H. Belk as long as he should live and "in such manner as he sees fit."

It further provided "That my brother, W. H. Belk, as such manager, is authorized and empowered to donate not exceeding 15 per cent of the profits derived from said business to benevolent institutions or charity, or to do such things as he may see fit, and I ratify and approve such donations and earnestly request my said four daughters"—the four unmarried daughters had been named as heirs to receive the Monroe business—"as partners of his to permit him from time to time to carry out this request."

A tribute to Dr. Belk in the Durham *Morning Herald* spoke of him as "one of the state's most successful business men. Noted chiefly as a merchant, in which business he was preeminently successful, his interests, particularly in his later years, touched almost every business and industry of his section. He was financially interested in many widely established enterprises and was on the official boards of many of them. He was a successful builder and his efforts have helped to make his section and the country more progressive and prosperous.

"As a merchant, associated with his brother, W. H. Belk, of Charlotte," the editorial continued, "he was at the head of 48 department stores, located in North and South Carolina, Virginia and Tennessee. This has been a constantly growing group for thirty years and only recently expanded into Tennessee. W. H. Belk started the first Belk store in Monroe. . . . They had very little capital but an abundance of energy and faith in their growing section and they determined to grow with it and they have been growing ever since.

"Success in business did not lead Dr. Belk to forget his duties as a citizen and churchman and he always bore a large share in the civic and religious duties of his community," this editorial went on. "Together with his brother he was largely responsible for the establishment of a hospital in Monroe and together they endowed and operated through the Presbyterian Church Board, a mission hospital in China. These are two conspicuous examples of many benefactions from a man who, though rich and powerful, never lost his simplicity of manner, nor his interest in the people of his community and section."

Mr. Belk recently summed up this relationship in his own homely way.

"Brother John and I always got along mighty well together. He had fine judgment about things and he always considered both sides of a situation before he made up his mind. Whatever he did always suited me, and I think whatever I did generally suited him. I suppose we were much closer than the average pair of brothers. Brother John was a good man, and a great man. I still miss him."

16

HENRY BELK DOES NOT CLAIM THAT HE PREDICTED THE
great depression. But by the time it came he had seen a number of them, big and little, and he had learned to distrust the
good times that come too easily. It is not surprising that, well
before the stock market crash that set off the depression, he
was cutting down his forward commitments and advising the
managers of the Belk stores to do likewise.

The depression is so much a matter of vivid personal memory to most readers of today that it is unnecessary to recount
the steps that led from 1929 to 1933. It was much the worst

depression in the country's history, simply because America had grown so much bigger, and the relations between farmer, laborer, industrialist, and business man were so much closer and more complex. There were no shelters against the storm. For Henry Belk, the worst part of it was that the bank failures across the land, the closing of countless business enterprises, the frightful drop in employment, the tremendous and often despairing efforts of business men everywhere to keep their organizations in existence—all these calamities as they affected the fortunes of the Belk stores had to be met and solved by himself alone without the calm good judgment of the partner upon whom he had come to rely so heavily.

Nor was he to be spared a further heavy personal blow. Almost at the pit of the depression—on March 9, 1932—Sarah Walkup Belk Simpson died. She was ninety-five at the time of her death and had retained her faculties almost to the last. She had been the source of much of Henry Belk's strength, and his weekly visits to go to church with her in Monroe had become a sustaining ritual in his life. He had sought her counsel on innumerable matters of importance to him and had all but worshipped her through the long years they had been together. Separation from her would affect him profoundly, and on every possible occasion hereafter he would recall her and take delight in honoring her memory. His consolation would be in his own family—in his wife and the five sons and one daughter of his marriage.

Whatever the personal loss, Henry Belk had to carry the major part of the burdens of the stores in the crisis that faced them. How well he carried them can be summed up in a brief but amazing statement of fact. Not a single Belk store closed its doors during the period; not only that, but the system expanded more rapidly in the number of new stores added during the three years from 1930 through 1932 than in any previous three-year period in its history.

Of course, there were probably few businesses of its size in the country in better condition to meet the depression. The Belk expansion in the twenties had been solid, resting on a shrewd choice of locations and an amazing ability at picking people. And there had been no involvement in New York financing, no speculative ventures to cover. The Belk stores could stand on their own feet. If you ask Mr. Belk about it, he will say simply that a good merchant can do a profitable business at any price level, provided he runs on a cash basis and does not allow himself to get loaded with goods bought at prices too high for the prevailing market.

But none of that can detract from the extraordinary calmness, courage, and confidence in the future of his country that Henry Belk exhibited in that despairing period. When business leaders of all types and statures were in a panic of apprehension about what the future held, he went about his business in picking new locations, selecting the right new men, and betting his money on the future. In 1932, at the very bottom of the depression, he was saying to J. Grier Hudson, a brother of Karl Hudson and then assistant manager of the Raleigh store:

"Grier, if I were a young man like you I wouldn't want any better opportunity than to locate in Spartanburg, one of the main textile centers of the South."

Mr. Hudson took his advice, and the store in Spartanburg that he took over became one of the best in the Belk-Hudson group.

But however great his confidence, it was not any easy time. For instance, when the Roosevelt administration was ushered in with the bank holiday, the Belk stores stayed open, even though Henry Belk had to arrange for private truck delivery of cash to some of them to tide them over. But for the whole period of the depression the total sales figures of the stores tell the story. In 1927, the thirty-nine stores that comprised the group did a total business of around twelve million dollars. In 1932, the seventy-nine stores of the expanded group did a total business of thirteen million dollars. Obviously the individual stores had suffered serious declines in their business; but Henry Belk had managed, by being willing to bet on the future, to keep the group as a whole expanding.

As in the earlier short depression in 1921, there were calls upon Henry Belk for help by many of the distressed industries in which he had an interest. This time there were many more, because the crisis was worse and his interests were wider. He will not talk of it himself, but his close associates can name a number of textile companies, since grown great, that managed to get through the depression on the basis of notes indorsed by Henry Belk. It was not blind charity, but it was a demonstration of his fundamental confidence in his region and his country. And it was typical of Henry Belk that he was willing to help those who helped themselves. The textile companies that he assisted were those seeking to pull through by getting machinery to produce new types of highly styled fabrics that had recently been developed. Henry Belk was thinking of the future.

When businessmen and the public regained their confidence in 1933 and 1934, it was natural that the Belk stores, seasoned and made confident by the experience of the depression, should be ready for a great expansion, and this was the case. Between 1933 and America's entry into the Second World War, one hundred and eleven new stores were added to the seventy-nine existing in 1932. North Carolina and South Carolina remained the area of greatest concentration, but many new stores appeared in Virginia, Georgia, and Tennessee; and Florida and Alabama appeared for the first time on the Belk map. And as in the twenties, the expansion avoided the big cities, Atlanta and Birmingham and Richmond and Norfolk, and centered on the small cities and towns. In spreading over the South, the Belk stores were attaining the character of the South, which today is moving away from its rural past, but is far from being a region dominated by cities.

Obviously, with the total number of stores heading toward two hundred, the Belk family of stores was far too large for the kind of close personal contact that Henry Belk had maintained with individual stores in the old days. But now the training that Henry Belk and John Belk had given the young men of the generation before began to show its greatest value. New stores continued to be established by Henry Belk from his Charlotte office, each in collaboration with some promising younger man who had developed under his eye. But most of the new stores were now being headed by the men whom the Belks had set up earlier and who had in turn trained young men for further expansion contemplated. From Mr. Belk's point of view, there was nothing complicated about it:

"We'd find a young man in one of our stores who was smart and ambitious, and we'd set him up in a store that he could run. Maybe he'd have some money saved up, and we'd lend him some more and put up some of the money ourselves. Then after he'd been going on along a good while and had learned a lot of merchandising, he'd probably discover that there was a smart young man in his store who would likely make a merchant on his own. He'd tell us about it, and pretty soon we'd all get together—the man who was part owner and manager of the store, the young man working for him who wanted to start his own business, and myself—we'd get together and look over the situation, and if things looked promising enough, we'd agree on a proposition, and the young man would open a new store. That's the way it went."

It was as simple in principle as Mr. Belk puts it, but a great deal more complicated in practice. That is why a list of the Belk stores is rather bewildering in its complexity of names and combinations of names. For the unique characteristic and superiority of the Belk system—if indeed it can be called a system—is that it allows all kinds of variations, but always worked out around the basic idea that the man who manages the individual store either is a part owner or has it well within his power to become one.

The easiest way to show the system at work is to hear the stories of some of the men who have become heads of leading groups within the big Belk group. W. E. Gallant is typical—we have already seen him as a young man being trained in the Charlotte store under the eye of Henry Belk.

"When I first went to Charlotte to work for the Belk stores, I thought I would probably just work there until school took up in the fall," Mr. Gallant said in a recent interview. "I had just finished high school, and I was undecided whether or not to go to college. I liked the retail business from the beginning, and Mr. Belk seemed to think that I was a pretty good salesman, so I just stayed on in the Charlotte store for thirteen years. When I left that store I was manager and buyer of the department that handled the better piece goods, linens, and other such staples.

"Mr. Belk knew that I was anxious to get a store and had been for several years. One day he came to me.

" 'Erskine,' he said, 'any time now you might start looking around for a good location for a store.'

"That was just what I wanted, of course. So I started looking. I looked over a part of North Carolina and a part of Virginia, and practically all of South Carolina, and finally I decided to come down here to Anderson. We opened here in April, 1919, in a store with a thirty-foot front, a hundred and twenty feet deep, two stories.

"At that time my brother Paul was bookkeeper for the Belk store in Charlotte. I suggested that he come along with me.

He did, and he stayed here for five or six years, and then we opened our second store, with Paul in charge."

That was the beginning of the expansion of the Gallant-Belk Company into a group within the Belk system. And like the Belk system generally, it was not planned and blueprinted from the beginning.

"When we first came to Anderson," Mr. Gallant continued his account, "I really had not thought much about how many stores we might eventually have. I had hoped that we would have more than one, but I hadn't expected that we would ever build up a group of thirty-five stores.

"One of the most important things to be considered in opening a store is the sort of manager you have. You must have one who is thoroughly trained and capable if you are to succeed. It is our policy—and I learned it with Mr. Belk —to train these managers in our own stores, and if we find that they are capable, wide awake, and trustworthy, it is our policy for them to have stock in certain of our stores.

"The Belk stores are operated, of course, as parts of a system. In most ways, however, they are operated as individual stores. It is up to the manager, for instance, to buy the class of merchandise that he thinks he can sell in his particular town. Mr. Belk allows his partners and managers to use their own judgment in most cases. About the only thing that he requires of all the Belk managers is that they conduct themselves in the proper manner at all times, that they have the right kind of merchandise on their shelves and counters, and that they treat their employees and customers right. And, of course, if a manager does this, there is no question but that he will have a profitable business.

"All of the Belk stores try to have as nearly as possible the same kinds of staple merchandise, and we try to have nearly the same prices. But in some towns you will find Belk stores carrying certain lines of merchandise that you do not find in Belk stores in other towns. If a Belk store has merchandise that becomes soiled or shopworn, it is up to the manager to get rid of it quickly, and he does not have to take this up with anyone. The store manager is the judge as to whether an item is to be marked down if it is not selling or is old, shopworn merchandise. If a store manager is not capable of doing this, then he is not capable of managing a store."

The Anderson merchant is convinced that the Belk system offers the kind of freedom that attracts the ambitious young man.

"As an example," he added, "I will mention my brothers. Paul M. Gallant has stock in our Anderson store, our Greenwood store, and also in the stores at Edgefield and Ware Shoals. He manages the Greenwood store and supervises the operation of the Ware Shoals and Edgefield stores. Paul, as I said, is the one who was bookkeeper in the Charlotte store and came with me when I opened up at Anderson.

"My brother James G. Gallant graduated from Davidson College and spent three years in the Virginia Medical College at Richmond. But after going to medical school three years, he decided, as Dr. John M. Belk had done, that he would rather be a merchant than a doctor, and so we put him in our Athens, Georgia, store for training. He had already worked in the Belk store in Charlotte during summer vacations and holidays, and that's probably where he got the idea that he'd like to be a merchant. Well, after we sent him to the Athens store for training, we made him manager of the Elberton, Georgia, store for a short time and then later, when we opened up a store in La Grange, Georgia, we made him manager of it. Still later we opened stores at Newnan, West Point, Covington, Manchester, and Hogansville, all in Georgia, and Roanoke, Alabama, and my brother James has stock in all of these and supervises their operation."

But success with Mr. Gallant's group has been earned by

many persons who are not relatives, Mr. Gallant hastened to point out.

"There is Mr. F. E. McHugh, for instance, who came to work for us here in Anderson just after the First World War," he said. "He worked here for a number of years and when we decided to open our store in Elberton, we sent him over there as manager. About a year later we opened the store in Athens, Georgia, where my brother James later took his training in the mercantile business, and we sent Mr. McHugh there as manager, and later we sold him stock in the new store. A few years later we opened a store in Commerce, Georgia, which he supervises, and last year we opened one in Madison, which Mr. McHugh also supervises and has stock in. He is a real showman—and that's a good trait for a merchant to have. When we built the new Athens store, we had a vacant third floor when we first moved in, which he turned into a great pony circus, with Santa Claus presiding. I heard that he even got a baby elephant up the freight elevator for the circus. You can bet he did a big Christmas business.

"Another young man who has made good with the Belk stores is Mr. R. V. Murray. Mr. Murray worked several years in our Burlington, North Carolina, store, and then we brought him down to Gainesville, Georgia, where he acted as salesman, window trimmer, and assistant manager. He was there a few years, and then when we opened our store in Toccoa, Georgia, in September, 1937, Mr. Murray was made manager and owned some of the stock. Later we opened stores at Cornelia, Georgia, in November, 1940, and at Clarksville, Georgia, in 1947, and Mr. Murray has stock in those businesses and supervises their operations. And now he is also supervising the stores at Hartwell, Georgia, and Royston, Georgia.

"I could name many other young men who have advanced rapidly with our stores," Mr. Gallant continued. "Garland

BELK's, Columbia, South Carolina

LEGGETT's DEPARTMENT STORE, South Boston, Virginia

BELK-LEGGETT COMPANY, Durham, North Carolina (*credit Parnell Studio*)

BELK-HUDSON COMPANY, Greenwood, Mississippi

Smith, for instance. He got his first training in the Gallant-Belk store in Gainesville, and when we opened the store in Seneca, South Carolina—that was in September, 1939—we sold him some stock in this store and made him manager. Now he is managing that store and supervising the management of two others. And had he not spent four or five years in the army, no doubt he would by now have had interests in several others.

"One day some years ago—eight or ten years—Garland Smith told me that a young man who was then working for one of our competitors in Seneca wanted to come with our store. The young man was Frank R. Chastain.

"I didn't advise Mr. Smith to offer young Chastain a job, because I didn't want to incur the ill will of this competitor. But not long after that I found out that Mr. Chastain had quit his job with this competitor and was working in our Seneca store. Not long afterwards the war started and Mr. Smith went into the army. We made Mr. Chastain manager of our Seneca store. And then when Mr. Smith came back after the war he resumed his position of manager and we transferred Mr. Chastain to Winder, Georgia, as manager of that store. Now Mr. Chastain is managing that store and supervising the management of the stores at Monroe, Lawrenceville, and Decatur, Georgia, and has stock in several of these stores.

"So there is plenty of opportunity for advancement for a young man in the Belk organization," Mr. Gallant summarized his discussion. "These I have mentioned are some of the men who have gone ahead. We have several other young men who are showing signs of becoming real merchants, and it is our policy to promote them in various ways just as fast as possible.

"As for the Belk stores generally, I feel that a Belk store in a community is a real asset. I think that good churches come first in any community, then good schools, and then good stores. One very important Belk policy is not to change managers every few years like many of the chain stores do. We try to encourage each manager to become a responsible and contributing citizen in the community in which he lives, and it is not our policy to change him unless we can give him a promotion to some larger responsibility.

"It is Mr. Belk's policy also—and mine, likewise—to do everything possible to see that the Belk store in any community is the best store there. Nor is there any reason why it shouldn't be. It is not our policy to play second fiddle to anyone. For that reason we insist on having stores large enough to carry just about everything anyone might want. We carry a full line of merchandise, everything for men, women, and children to wear, and also house furnishings. We want enough space at all times to display merchandise properly. In fact, we have always contended that good merchandise, well bought and well displayed, was already half sold.

"And in regard to the type of merchandise the Belk stores sell, it has been our policy to offer merchandise cheap enough for anyone but good enough also for the most discriminating customer. We take pride in the fact, though, that regardless of how much or how little a customer may pay for an article in our stores, it must be worth the price he pays. And we stand behind everything we sell. It is not our policy to allow anyone to undersell us on anything. We believe in small profits but fast turnovers."

Mr. Gallant declared he was confident that no merchandising organization in the nation was able to buy goods at lower prices than the Belk stores.

"We buy direct from the biggest mills in the country," he declared, "and there is no quantity of merchandise offered us that is too small or too large for us to buy. If the quantity is small, one store may handle it, or if it is larger, ten stores may use it, or forty or fifty, or a hundred. We may have the opportunity to buy some special close-out merchandise in such quantity that it may be enough for all the stores; if it isn't enough to go around, we divide it among those stores that want it. We are always looking for quality merchandise that we can buy under price so that in turn we can sell it to our customers for less than regular price."

Mr. Gallant, like Mr. Belk, gets a genuine thrill of enjoyment out of selling things.

"There is something about the merchandising business that gets you," he declared. "There is nothing I enjoy more than getting in the car and visiting the other stores and discussing merchandising with the managers of these stores and the others who work in them. All of us are always open to new suggestions and new ideas for improving our stores and our service to our communities."

The Gallant-Belk store in Anderson, like the Gallant-Belk system itself and the Belk family of stores generally, has grown tremendously in the thirty years since Mr. Gallant opened for business there.

"We had that one building, thirty by a hundred and twenty, two stories high," Mr. Gallant replied. "Now we have five buildings with a frontage of a hundred and fifty feet, all of them two hundred feet deep, with first and second floors and basements under all of them, which gives us something over eighty thousand square feet of floor space."

Mr. Gallant's sons, like Mr. Belk's, are likely to follow their father in directing Belk stores, he forecast.

"My son Erskine, Jr., will graduate from Duke University next spring and it is my hope and expectation that he will go into the stores as soon as he gets out of school," he said. "Robert, my youngest son, went to Davidson two years and then to the University of North Carolina. He is expecting to go into the stores just as soon as he graduates—if he does not have to go into the army, at any rate, as soon as he can.

"The Belk stores, I repeat, offer a great opportunity to the young man who is willing to work, anxious to learn, and ambitious to get ahead."

Arthur L. Tyler is another head of a group within the larger Belk family whose story is revealing; it points up the Belk story the more so because Mr. Tyler is one of the few Belk leaders who did not get his training in a Belk store. Mr. Tyler, a Virginian, started his career as a merchant at the age of twelve with the Henderson, North Carolina, unit of the Anchor chain stores.

"Even though I was just a small boy—a twelve-year-old youngster in knee pants—I was the oldest boy in a family of six children and it had become necessary for me to help with the family budget and also assist in the education of my brothers and sisters. For this reason it was impossible for me to get a complete college education, although I was fortunate in having one year at the University of North Carolina. And the assistance I was able to give other members of my family has always been one of my greatest joys as I look back on my youth. It has been a source of much pride to have five sisters and brothers, all of them college graduates as a result of my labors."

His early experience in the department store field, he recalls, was usually interesting but not without "problems and vicissitudes," as he expresses it.

"I led a life of variety, all right. Janitor work, errand boy, card writer, salesman, display man—those were some of my jobs. In fact, I was called upon to do almost anything that came to hand. My hours usually ran from 7:30 in the morning until 7:00 at night, and many Saturdays found me at the store after midnight.

"I always tried, though, to do my work well, and my experience as the years rolled by proved that there was always room just ahead. Finally I was made head of the Anchor chain's store in Winston-Salem."

It was after he had moved to Winston-Salem, he reveals, that he began to fear that he had reached the end of his opportunity to advance in the merchandising field.

"At this point, I was approached by Mr. Frank Stevens, one of the moving spirits of the Belk group of stores," he continues. "I'll never forget that day. It was raining, I remember, and on top of that, business was somewhat depressing, too. That day Mr. Stevens asked me if I would go over for an interview with Mr. Belk. I told him I would be glad to.

"During my long years with the Belk organization I have many times thought back over my first conversation with Mr. Belk," he went on. "I well remember that as soon as I entered his office I began to be impressed with his genuineness and warm cordiality. He seemed from that first moment I saw him to be a man of simple honesty. Nor will I ever forget his first remarks to me. I can hear him right now as he started off.

" 'Well, Frank Stevens tells me that you are a pretty good man and have been giving him quite a bit of competition over here in Winston-Salem,' he said.

"I thanked him for this recognition. Then his very next words were:

" 'Mr. Tyler, are you a Christian?'

"I told him that I had always tried to lead a Christian life.

" 'Well,' he asked me then, 'are you a Presbyterian?'

"I felt my stock slipping then because I was an Episcopalian. But I don't suppose that fact hurt my chances with him. I do remember well though how much his conversation and his general attitude impressed me, and I felt that any man who was so earnestly interested in his church must necessarily be a good man.

"Well, the interview that day was a very satisfactory one and I decided to go with the Belk organization. As a result of the conference I moved down to Rocky Mount to start my first venture with the Belk stores. Time has certainly proved the wisdom of my decision, and my connection with Mr. Belk has been a happy and successful one."

Mr. Tyler's first job was that of reorganizing a Belk store in Rocky Mount, North Carolina, with the new name of the Belk-Tyler Company.

"I came to Rocky Mount in March, 1931, and after everything had moved along in a smooth manner for a year or so we opened the second unit of our group at Goldsboro. A Belk store had been operating there for several years, but an impossible upturn in the lease made it impracticable to continue the store longer. One day the telephone rang and immediately I recognized the voice of Mr. Henry.

" 'I am over at Goldsboro right now,' he said. 'Can't you run over for a few minutes?'

"I assured him that I would be there in forty minutes. And when I got to the store in Goldsboro I found Mr. Henry out in front looking dejectedly at the store windows. They were plastered with signs:

GOING OUT OF BUSINESS SALE!
WE CANNOT RENEW OUR LEASE.
GOOD-BYE, GOLDSBORO!

" 'Now look at those signs, Arthur,' Mr. Henry said, as soon as he had greeted me. 'They make me sick. You know I open stores, not close them! I have never closed a store in my life!'

"That made a lasting impression on me; 'I open stores, not close them!' That same day we surveyed the city for another location and before I left that afternoon another location had been found and we had signed a lease. That was the beginning of the second Belk-Tyler store—in September, 1934. It was the beginning, too, of the expansion of our group, for as fast as men could be developed to assume managerial posts, we started opening the new Belk-Tyler stores. The third store was opened in Tarboro, also in September, 1934, and this was followed by the opening of the store at Elizabeth City in March, 1935; then Kinston was opened in March, 1936, and Washington in August, 1936; next was Farmville, opened in January, 1937; then followed Williamston in March, 1937; Ahoskie, in September, 1937; Greenville was next, in August, 1938; and in March, 1942, the Wilson store opened for business. At the present time we are completing construction on the twelfth and thirteenth units in the Belk-Tyler group, the stores at Plymouth and Edenton."

Mr. Tyler believes that Mr. Belk's success may be attributed in large part to the fact that he understands people, and especially to the ability he has in selecting men.

"Much has been said about Mr. Belk's success as a merchant," said Mr. Tyler. "Yet I have found him always to be a quiet, modest man with a head full of good common 'horse sense,' always ready and eager to listen to the other man regardless of that man's station in life. Many times I have heard Mr. Belk say that a person can always get good ideas from the other fellow if he will only listen. And this is certainly true. Mr. Belk's success, as I see it, is the result of his keen knowledge of humanity, and his unerring faculty of being able to select a man capable of doing the job he is chosen to do. In this art he is a past master. If a man is able to establish himself in Mr. Belk's confidence, he will back him to the limit. He has always allowed the man working for him and with him to use his own brain, to formulate his own plans, and to operate his business—without interference.

"To my mind, these characteristics of Mr. Belk account largely for the outstanding success he has made. Many times I have heard him say to one of his men: 'Just back your judgment.' "

Any number of other stories of personal success within the Belk group could be added to the stories of Mr. Gallant and Mr. Tyler. There would be people like John Parks, a Union County boy trained in the Monroe store and who launched the first Belk store in Tennessee in 1928. With his brother, and later a second generation of Parkses, they built a group of thirteen Parks-Belk stores in Tennessee and Virginia. And there would be J. W. Hensdale, a "second generation" Belk man who trained under Frank Stevens in the Belk-Stevens store in Winston-Salem, and after thorough seasoning in Belk methods in several Belk-Stevens stores began his own Belk-Hensdale group with a store in Fayetteville, North Carolina. The Belk system has made many men well-to-do—it was designed to do so—but the important point to note is that the goal it has set for the young man beginning as a merchant is not a high-level job in a main office, but the opportunity to have a store, or group of stores, in which he has a real interest.

An example of an outstanding manager is George W. Dowdy of the Charlotte store, biggest of the nearly three hundred. Mr. Dowdy is the third man, not including Henry Belk himself, to direct the operations of this great mercantile institution. It is a coincidence that Mr. Dowdy as a young man entered the Belk organization the year the first manager died in 1919.

G. Herbert McDonald, a native Mecklenburger, as a boy got a job in the East Trade Street store when the Monroe merchant came to Charlotte to open his first branch establishment. Pneumonia cut short at forty a career in merchandising that already had been highly successful and robbed Charlotte's business and cultural life of a young man who had quickly become one of its most important civic leaders.

Mr. Dowdy entered merchandising in the employ of Belk's Durham store. His ability, initiative, and willingness to work were soon noticed, and after a period of training and seasoning in Durham he was sent to Concord as manager of the store in the Cabarrus capital. He held that post until he was advanced to the Charlotte store to succeed B. Frank Matthews, one of the principal Belk executives who had been managing the Charlotte business after the death of Mr. McDonald.

Mr. Dowdy in early 1956 was one of four American business leaders sent by the Department of Commerce on a seven-week mission to Italy to encourage the exchange of goods between Italy and the United States.

The Belk operations in Charlotte have always been profitable. Despite the depression with its lean years of the early thirties, the volume of business in that city continued to expand and soon the greatly enlarged store of 1927 was becoming inadequate. Another large addition was planned and in 1938, little more than a decade after the opening of the 120,000 square-foot structure that the Belk leaders thought would be adequate for many years of developing business, the remodeled store was opened to a rush of customers. It now extended from East Trade Street through the block to East Fifth Street and contained 190,000 square feet of floor space. The store was the largest in the Carolinas.

But within another decade this structure too was becoming inadequate. Henry Belk, George Dowdy, and their associates in Charlotte began giving consideration to preliminary plans for a greatly enlarged building that would virtually double the floor space of the 1938 store.

The success of the Charlotte store may be attributed in large measure to the initiative and ability of its leadership. But also a largely contributing factor has been the faithfulness of long-time employees. Some have been mentioned; many others could be, among them the late Walter L. Wallis, manager of piece goods; Raymond D. Currence, merchandising manager; John D. Elliott, manager of men's wear; Miss Hattie Robinson, in charge of sales records; Miss Rebecca Elliott, in charge of boys' and students' clothing and furnishings.

17

THE DECADE FROM 1932 TO 1942 MARKED THE EMER-
gence of the Belk family of stores as big business by any
American standard. The figures tell the story. In 1932, com-
piled records show, 88 stores did a business of thirteen
million dollars; five years later in 1937, there were 154
stores and they did a business of between twenty-five and
fifty million dollars; and five years later, in 1942, 193 stores
of that period had pushed the volume of business done to
between one hundred and one hundred and fifty million dollars. The sales figures for the nearly 300 stores in 1949 are,

of course, proportionately higher because of the inflation of the dollar.

Becoming a giant did nothing to change the fundamental method of operation of the Belk group—and it had no visible effect on Henry Belk as a man. In 1942 he was eighty years old, though a visitor or acquaintance could never have suspected it; he had seen too much of life to be impressed by figures, even if they were in nine digits, and he was never a man given to boasting.

He was still very much the leader of the huge family of enterprises that he headed. He still liked to go on the floor in the Charlotte store. He still spent a big part of his time talking to the young managers who wanted his advice. The cracker-barrel kind of wisdom that had always characterized his talk is evident in the story of a young manager who came to him about this time with his buying problem.

"Mr. Belk," he said, "I'm pretty worried over how much I should buy for next season's selling."

"Why, son," he said to the young man, his tone quiet and gentle, "that's nothing to be worrying about. Just buy enough but don't buy too much."

Another story of this period is evidence of the real value he put on big success. An old friend had dropped by his office to see him and the talk turned to his achievements.

"I have five boys and one girl," he said, and his pride in them was evident in his voice. "They are all pretty smart, too, if I do say it. Not a numbskull in the bunch. I think they'll make their way all right. And I'd like to see them all well-off some day. But—" he tapped the desk top with the palm of his hand—"I'd a lot rather see them as poor as Job's turkey and good Christians than the other way around. That's what counts most—far more than any money you might make —being a good Christian."

The people who know Mr. Belk best are certain that

this statement expresses a literal truth about Henry Belk's feelings.

One change was necessary in the over-all procedures of the Belk stores, and it was not a departure from previous practice but a formal recognition of a gradual change that had taken place over the years. Through the years the Charlotte store had been acting in an informal way as a sample display house for all the Belk stores, and the fifth floor of the building had been devoted to this purpose. Through the years, too, the Charlotte store had provided other aids to the stores of the Belk family. As far back as 1920 a traffic office had been set up in the Charlotte store, to handle problems of the delivery of merchandise. At the same time, the Charlotte store had employed a tax expert to advise and assist the store managers on the tax problems facing them.

By 1940, the size of the group was such that something more formal was needed. That was the origin of the Belk Buying Service, which was set up then as an agency of all the Belk stores. It took over all the central purchasing functions as well as the other services that had been developed as a part of the Charlotte store operation, including the real estate advisory service that had been set up in 1939. A new building was planned for the Buying Service, but the war intervened before it could be started, and it was not until 1949 that the handsome new building on East Fifth Street in Charlotte was completed. The New York office also continues its expanded and vital function in its great market.

The Second World War was a terrific added burden to a man whose business had grown to giant size. Particularly to a person as conscientious as Henry Belk, such problems as were posed by price control, the strict allocation of materials, and the black market were continuous headache. The controls were necessary for victory, and they were strictly observed throughout the Belk group, but they were completely counter to the Belk way of doing business, which had always depended upon a free market for the man with the best sense of the bargains that the public would want. Belk expansion in the war period was naturally much reduced; in the four years 1942 through 1945, only thirty new stores were added. It would have been a notable expansion at an earlier period, but in comparison with the growth of the thirties, it was a slowing up. Many of the places in which new stores were opened were towns in which war industries and military training had swelled the population and created a desperate need, as well as an opportunity, for new stores, but it is a commentary on the shrewdness of Henry Belk and the heads of the various Belk groups that the locations they chose were not simply war-boom towns. Not one of the stores opened during the war have been closed since.

Like so many other businesses, the Belk group was ready for the opening of new business as soon as the war was over, and 1946 was the year of the biggest expansion in Belk history. Twenty-eight new stores—one every two weeks—swelled the area embraced. They added to the total of the stores in each of the states in which there had been Belk stores before and moved into new territory in Kentucky, Maryland, Mississippi, and even established a solitary outpost in Ohio—Ironton. And among the eleven stores chartered the following year was the Belk-Jones Company in Texarkana, Arkansas-Texas. Henry Belk, more than a half century after he had first thought of doing it, had finally gone into business in Texas.

With the ending in 1950 of the first half of the century the total number of Belk stores had grown to two hundred and ninety, operating in every state of the South from Maryland to the Rio Grande. The man who had started three quarters of a century before as a country merchant in Monroe, North Carolina, truly could call himself merchant of the South.

VI

A MERCHANT'S DEMOCRACY

A. W. Harry, Salisbury, North Carolina (*credit Manning Studio*)

Belk-Hensdale Company, Fayetteville, North Carolina

A. F. STEVENS, Winston-Salem, North Carolina

J. C. WILLIAMS, Wilmington, North Carolina

18

HENRY BELK MIGHT BE ABLE TO NAME THE YEARS WHEN the volume of sales of all the Belk stores first reached a million dollars a year—or five million, or ten million. According to his associates, he is a man who, on any day of the year, could give you out of his head a fairly accurate financial picture of any one of the nearly three hundred stores in the Belk group. But the figures on the over-all business of the group are in his head alone. They are not matters of public record, and there is no inside group of stockholders who know them. For there is no one corporation in control of the stores, and

Mr. Belk is the only man who is a stockholder in nearly all of them. There has never been any occasion for the compiling of sales volume records. Mr. Belk is the last man in the world to want to boast about sales figures, and good Scotch-Irish canniness has made him chary of giving figures to the idly curious. The few total sales figures given in this volume are the first authenticated figures that he has permitted to be made public.

This fact emphasizes the unique nature of the basic scheme upon which the Belk system of stores has been built. The best way to describe the Belk group is to liken it to a family. The nearly three hundred stores might be described as brothers and sisters, each an individual, each independent and living his own life, yet each related to the others by certain family traits and characteristics, and each under the authority or advice, however vigilant and strict or relaxed and unasserted, of the father of the family.

When Dr. John Belk was living, the Belk brothers were the head of this family of stores. Now Henry Belk is the man around whom the much enlarged family gathers. He is the hub into which the spokes of the great Belk wheel are fastened. This wheel, with the hub in Charlotte, extends outward to a rim that circles from Ohio to Texas and back along the Atlantic coastal towns to Maryland, and the spokes are getting closer and closer together as new stores are opened in promising territory.

The Belk stores generally are divided into two principal categories, the single stores, of which there are more than sixty, roughly between a fifth and a fourth of the entire number, and the others that are divided into the various subgroupings. Many of the larger stores are in the first category, among them those in Charlotte, Columbia, Charleston, Savannah, Winston-Salem, Greensboro, the parent store at Monroe, and many others.

The other stores are divided among more than two dozen groups. In a number of instances the group is headed by a man who has come up from long experience in a Belk store that has become the parent of the group. In other instances the group may have split into several smaller groups headed by brothers or sons or other relatives or associates of the man who originally headed the group as co-owner-manager. The independence of the individual store, however, is maintained within the general family of Belk stores.

The Charlotte office maintains space for a buying office in New York, staffed with some fifty specialists in merchandising, particularly the fast-moving, seasonable high-priced goods that must be bought quickly and sold quickly before changing styles may make them obsolete. Its services are available to all the Belk stores. And working for the Belk stores as a group, as has been pointed out, is the Belk Buying Service in Charlotte, staffed with an even larger force of specialists in every type of merchandise and in all other needs of a vast selling organization.

Mr. Belk's and his sons' offices are in this building, as are the offices of David M. McConnell, general counsel of the stores, and his assistants, E. A. Anderson, controller, the senior buying executives, and others whose work covers the entire field of Belk selling and servicing. At first look it might appear that this is the busy headquarters of a great chain. How can nearly three hundred stores co-operate to the advantage of each without being, in fact if not in fiction, a chain-store system or a unitary group? But distinctly they are not.

Why? In the first place, a chain-store system is an entity. Its corporate structure makes it so. The Belk stores are no entity. They are individual stores, individually owned. There is no corporate structure uniting them and stock ownership proportions are a crazy quilt of variation.

Again, a chain store is centrally managed and directed.

From headquarters, usually in New York, orders go out each day perhaps, or each week, to the various store managers; from the central headquarters even prices of merchandise are set, reductions in prices are ordered, sales are planned, selling campaigns are arranged, and inventories controlled. But no such orders go out to Belk managers from Charlotte. No plans for sales are made, no directions are given for control of inventories, no managers are told what to do and what not to do. In most cases the managers are substantial part-owners of the business; they are not managers in the usual chain-store sense. In most stores—though not all—Henry Belk or members of his family or his brother's family are majority owners; if an actual clash of views over the operation of a store should develop, Mr. Belk or the other majority owners of the stock could legally tell the minority owner-manager what to do in a properly called corporate meeting. But not as the head of a chain store, it should be emphasized. They could put their wishes into effect only as majority owners of stock in that one store. Their position as majority owners of stock in other stores would have nothing to do with the situation within that one store.

What then is the Belk Buying Service and why should there be any need of such a service? That is a proper question anyone interested in the detailed story of the Belk stores might wish answered.

Belk's Buying Service is in reality the office which Mr. Belk maintains to discharge the functions which have been delegated to him by the several stores. In providing a centralized buying service, the stores are enabled not only to obtain merchandise at the most favorable prices available, but also it enables each store, large or small, to have the benefit of the advice of purchasing specialists who spend their entire time in their separate fields in product research, comparison, and pricing and style developments. Originated only for purchasing, this technique has been extended to other aspects of management, and now stores have direct access to specialized assistance on problems of accounting, auditing and bookkeeping, legal and corporate organization, real estate transactions, construction and remodeling plans, and traffic management.

To perform these functions, Mr. Belk has brought together to aid him in serving the stores:

S. H. Scott, piece goods and textiles, and learning this field under his supervision, Tom Belk, youngest son of Mr. Belk. Mr. Scott is one of the canniest operators in his field in the nation and an industrialist and philosopher whose techniques and outlook are a byword in the trade;

B. Frank Matthews, men's and boys' wear, former manager of the Charlotte store, and one of the veterans of the Belk organization, known as a beloved leader by the entire trade;

A. P. Craddock, formerly of the Craddock-Terry Shoe Company of Lynchburg, Virginia, one of the nation's authorities in his field—shoes;

David M. McConnell, a specialist in taxation and corporate organization and a former attorney for the United States Commissioner of Internal Revenue, who is general counsel for each of the stores and therefore available to any who may wish his counsel on any matters of a legal nature;

J. W. Cunningham, hosiery, another veteran of the Belk organization and long an expert in that division of merchandising;

Sam C. Elliott, boys' wear, long with the Belk organization and highly proficient in his field;

Miss Martha Shields, another veteran, lingerie, with Miss Sarah Belk, Mr. Belk's only daughter, as her understudy;

John M. Belk, second son of Mr. Belk, co-ordinator of the various purchasing policies and programs;

D. J. Bostian, eighty-three and almost as old as Mr. Belk,

still keenly aware of his field's developing opportunities, housewares and notions;

E. A. Anderson, a veteran of a score of years service with the Belk stores, controller;

Gibson L. Smith, real estate, whose office aids any store in any real estate problem that may arise;

W. A. Gilliland, central billing and office supply purchasing, a function of considerable importance in an organization as large as the Belk stores family;

W. J. Smith, traffic bureau chief, who heads a staff whose duties are to arrange the quickest and most economical routes for the shipment of goods to the stores;

L. O. Puckett, in charge of the building and engineering department, which directs construction and maintenance of buildings;

Two other principal specialists, William Henry Belk, Jr., and Irwin Belk, assist their father in financing operations of the organization in behalf of the various stores, in addition to their responsibility as directors of many of the stores. Henderson Belk, the fourth son, served for a time as manager of the Asheville store, which gave him excellent training for the larger responsibility of personnel director of the Belk stores. His daughter Sarah early became interested in ready-to-wear, an apprenticeship that would help fit her to have charge of that important phase of the store's business.

These and all of the other people in the Belk Buying Service work closely, day by day, with the buyers and managers of the stores, both in the Buying Service Building and in the field. Their spirit of friendliness and cooperation is especially engendered by the feeling that each of them is a part of the staff of each of the stores.

19

H ENRY BELK HAS HIS OWN HOMESPUN WAY OF EXPLAINING how his "system" works.

"Well," he will say, leaning back in his chair and rubbing the palms of his hands together, "I don't reckon we've got any system. We just sell goods. And sometimes we get along pretty well—generally do, in fact, but sometimes—" he will grin—"we don't do so well.

"I think what success we've had has been due in a large measure to the fact that the Belk stores are independent. I guess if we've got any plan at all that could be called distinctly our plan, that's it. We're citizens in a democracy—our stores, I mean. We're free and independent, but we try to work together to help each other out. That's what you're supposed to do in a democracy, isn't it? You see, the manager of a Belk store is pretty much on his own. Nobody in Charlotte or anywhere else tells him how to run it. He has a chance to show his mettle, and you know, a man—any man who's trying to do a good job and get ahead—likes that. You see this freedom of running their business gives them a chance to demonstrate their own individual merchandising abilities while at the same time under our way of doing business they are profiting by their association with the other stores in our organization.

"We've got two buying offices that were set up just to help the stores. They're a service, that's all. I didn't care about all this fanciness—" he will sweep his arm in a broad curve to indicate the walnut paneling, the thick carpet, the heavy draperies, the soft lights—"but Sarah and the boys wanted me to have it, and I told them to go ahead, though I wasn't used to this sort of fancy business.

"Well, as I was saying, these offices are for the benefit of the stores. The manufacturers can bring their merchandise here for us to see and they can display it here for the convenience of our various store managers. By coming here or visiting the office in New York they can keep in close touch with the latest trends in merchandising. Those who live in this part of the country can save a lot of time and considerable expense and can make more frequent visits to the Charlotte office than they could if they had to visit the markets in the north and east.

"And by coming here a Belk manager, regardless of how small his store is or in how small a place it may be, has the advantage of our service, which helps him keep up with every changing factor in the merchandising business. And the main thing, of course, is that it enables him to buy merchandise at the lowest prices and to have the help of specialists who keep in constant touch with merchandising opportunities.

"But although this is true," Mr. Belk will add, with considerable emphasis, "it's true, too, that each Belk manager doesn't have to buy his goods through this central buying service. No, sir, he doesn't have to do that. He can buy his goods wherever it's to his advantage to get them. He just uses the central buying service when its prices are better. It has to compete for his business along with everybody else.

"For example, if some store in a town where a Belk store is operating should decide to go out of business for one reason or another and should decide to sell out its stock at sacrifice prices, the Belk store manager in that town has every right to purchase that stock if it's to his advantage to do it. Probably the prices will be lower than those the buying office could quote him on the same sort of goods. Well, he should jump right in and buy that stuff.

"Or if a salesman on the road should come along with something the manager might want and at a good price, then he can buy from that salesman. And he doesn't have to call anybody for permission. He's supposed to take advantage of all the opportunities he can find. He's the manager. It's his job to run his store. In the case of the various big chain-store systems, this wouldn't be possible, certainly without the issuance of permits from the home office, and by the time all that telephoning or writing could be done, the opportunity of getting the stuff cheap would be gone. The Belk store manager in that way is always in position to strike a good deal. If he can get merchandise for one reason or another cheaper than he can through the buying service, then all the better it is. The Belk Buying Service, as I said, must compete with everybody else for his trade.

"But, on the other hand, if a store manager has some

problem bothering him and wants help, he can usually get it by writing, or better, by coming to see us. We've got specialists just to help him. We've got a legal department, headed by Mr. McConnell, that can help on a lot of problems, including such things as setting up corporations, certain tax problems, and many others involving legal questions, and all a store manager has to do is just ask for the help he wants. Mr. McConnell, Phi Beta Kappa man educated at Davidson College and Harvard Schools of Law and Business Administration and former secretary to James F. Byrnes, is the sort of young man that we have chosen for this era of government involvement in business.

"We have a real estate department under Mr. Gibson Smith that will help procure sites for stores, arrange for leases, and handle all matters concerned with real estate transactions. We've got an auditing department whose service is available to each of the stores. In fact, all these central departments are set up to contribute their specialists' abilities in solving problems of the store managers and others connected with the Belk organization. In these times, with the government impact on business, that kind of help is mighty important when the store manager feels that he needs a hand."

Mr. Belk's office in the Belk Buying Service building is at the left as one enters the handsome two-story and basement structure. The offices of other principal executives and the conference rooms are on this first floor. The basement provides a large assembly room and a tremendous storage area, and the second floor is devoted exclusively to the display of merchandise and offices of the chief merchandising or buying executives. Here in air-conditioned comfort Belk stores' buyers can see the latest-style goods displayed to best advantage. Indirect lighting of the display shelves and racks, the lavish use of color, the careful harmonizing of the goods being displayed with the fixtures and permanent furnishings of the

sections in which they are being shown—all have been devised with the single purpose of making the Belk Buying
Service unsurpassed—perhaps unequaled in the nation.

Mr. Belk, despite his complete lack of pretension, is very
proud of the handsome new building.

"I reckon," he agrees, "it ought to make it a lot easier
for us to sell more goods."

In the building, too, although entirely separate administra-
tively, is the office of the Belk Profit-Sharing Trusts, adminis-
tered by Mr. Joseph B. Simpson, a former revenue officer.

"We've had a lot of folks stay with us through the years,"
Mr. Belk says. "On the second floor of the Charlotte buying
office building are several rows of framed pictures of scores
of employees who have been with us a long time, some of them
for more than half a century. They're what you might call in
the family. We've all sort of grown up together. Most of our
folks stay on the job until they are well up in years. But now
when one of our men or women feels that it's time to start
taking things easier, we have funds of the employees' trusts
built up with money contributed entirely by the stores—
which now totals between four and five million dollars—that
permits such an employee, by adding this nest egg from
shared profits from the stores to his social security payments
and personal savings accumulated through the years, to have a
more comfortable old age."

At the end of the corridor that leads left to the offices of
Mr. Belk, his son Henry, and his son Irwin, is a small recep-
tion room presided over by Miss Sarah Caddell, who for
years has been Mr. Belk's secretary and who perhaps knows
as much as any one person other than Mr. Belk the Belk history, policies, and personnel. She has seen the Belk stores
increase by the scores, the Belk children grow up and assume
important duties in the organization, and the Belk volume

of sales double and redouble and double again and again.

In her very gracious and unobtrusive way she handles a multitude of duties, one of the most important of which is the arranging of Mr. Belk's engagements. And in his manner of receiving visitors Mr. Belk is again very much an individual.

Busy as he still is at the age of eighty-seven, Henry Belk is at the same time one of the most accessible of men. Not only to men and women of influence, but to anyone. Not a day passes that he does not have numerous visitors and often the day's list will include some old Negro seeking a little gift for his church, a young minister from some rural area who needs aid in carrying out some project in which he is interested, a committee from the presbytery or the synod, an old friend from down in the Waxhaw country, any one of countless members of the Belk personnel. There is no fuss and bother about getting in to see Mr. Belk. Miss Caddell will invariably arrange it in a moment's time.

But there's one time of the year when it is best not to call Miss Caddell for an appointment with Mr. Belk—unless the business is urgent. If toward the end of the year you should write or telephone for such an appointment, she will invariably suggest that you "try to see Mr. Henry before the end of the year or wait until after the middle of February; he's going to be mighty busy for the first six or seven weeks of the year."

That period, she will explain, embraces the "period when all the annual meetings of the stores are held," and it is the busiest time of the year in the program of the Belk organization, particularly at the headquarters office in Charlotte.

Perhaps no other office in the South, and few, if any, in the nation can be pointed out as the place in which as many directors' and stockholders' meetings are held as this Charlotte office of Henry Belk.

The procedure each year is virtually the same, except that

the period grows longer as the number of stores increases. A schedule of meetings is prepared, the schedule is sent out to the various stores, and the managers report on the days set for their respective annual meetings.

Mr. Belk as president of the store corporation whose annual meeting is being held calls the meeting to order and presides. The annual sessions are relatively informal, the business is straight to the point, there is no detailed folderol. The manager presents his report to the directors, the report is discussed briefly, any business that is pressing for attention is transacted, the stockholders meet and elect directors for the new year, the officers are named, and the new directors' meeting is shortly concluded. The next store meeting is called to order, its report is received, discussed, its annual business transacted, and the next is called. That is the procedure through a long business day, five days a week. Annual meetings are not held on Saturdays.

The 1949 schedule—the last series of meetings held in Mr. Belk's old office on the fourth floor of the Belk store in Charlotte—will serve to enlighten anyone interested in studying the unusual Belk method of holding the annual business meetings of this great group of stores.

The meetings began on Monday, January 3, and this opening day was devoted to the annual meeting of the Young Manufacturing Company, a store and bank fixture factory, one of a number of manufacturing enterprises headed by Mr. Belk.

The next day the stores at Statesville, Conway, Elkin, Sparta, and West Jefferson held their meetings. On Wednesday eight others—Mooresville, Union, Newton, Kings Mountain, Fort Mill, York, Rome, and Carrollton—were on the schedule. The following days the stores under the general direction of Ray Cline of Concord, fourteen stores in eleven cities, held their meetings. On Friday ten single, or independent, stores in four states transacted their business of the year.

That was the way the schedule was followed. On some days the number of meetings was larger, particularly when the big groups met. And the procedure of holding these meetings, too, further reveals the nature of the Belk system—an organization of nearly three hundred stores, some supervised and partially owned in groups, others single and independent, each independently managed, but all related to each other through their personal and business relationship to Henry Belk, the head of the family.

From the point of view of the president of a chain-store system, this rigidly followed legal procedure of the annual meetings must seem like the waste of a lot of valuable time for a busy executive. Why not turn in the stock, issue new stock in one big company, and settle the annual business in one day? If you want to be generous, give the good managers a commission on the earnings of their stores or a small block of stock in the big organization. That is the "efficient" way.

From Mr. Belk's point of view, nothing that he does during the year is more important than the time he spends on these meetings. In the first place, brief as they are—some of them especially—they are not mere formalities. They are his chance, at least once a year, to talk to most of the managers— and in his opinion the managers in the field, rather than the specialists in Charlotte and New York, are the real keys to the success of the group. Even more important, the meetings are the reality as well as the symbol of the independence of the individual store. Each is a business conference of a parliamentary and legal nature between the people most concerned in the success of an individual enterprise. It is not enough that a manager of a store be well treated. Even a yearly bonus based on the earnings of his store is too impersonal. And a block of stock in some parent company, whose total earnings have little relationship to the contribution of his store, gives the manager no sense of profiting from his own achievements. But a manager who is a part owner of his own enterprise, who can profit directly from his own effort, and who attends by his own right the highest policy meetings that concern his store—such a manager is a citizen with voting rights in a kind of merchant's democracy. Mr. Belk believes that it is worth all the time it takes him, and more, to maintain that kind of relationship in the great Belk family of stores.

20

HENRY BELK INSISTS MODESTLY THAT ANY YOUNG MAN of good character with a fair equipment of brains who is willing to work long and hard can attain success comparable to that he has had in the world of merchandising.

"You know," he will say, "it's no great trouble to make money running a store. Of course, nowadays with all the taxes it's hard to clear much. But a fellow can make money selling goods. The main thing it takes is character. I remember reading in the papers once that J. P. Morgan was asked if the banks didn't lend money mainly on a man's financial standing, on the money he had.

B. FRANK MATTHEWS, Charlotte, North Carolina, has been with the Belk stores fifty-eight consecutive years, the longest service record in the entire organization

BELK STORES SERVICE, INC., Charlotte, North Carolina

BELK'S DEPARTMENT STORE, Greensboro, North Carolina

BELK-ROBINSON COMPANY, Charleston, South Carolina

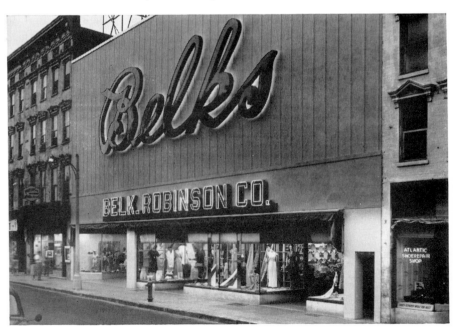

" 'No,' Morgan told them, 'I wouldn't lend a man a cent regardless of his financial standing if he didn't have character. Character is the principal thing.'

"And that's a fact. The main thing it takes to make a success in the merchandising business, just as it does in anything else, is character. A crook just won't make money. He may make it for a while, but he'll lose it. It won't stay with him."

Of course, Henry Belk has contributed a great deal more toward achieving his success than hard work alone. He is possessed of that peculiar sense that may be described, for the lack of a better term, as "knowing how to make a good trade." He has always enjoyed selling things, as he will invariably tell anyone who engages him in conversation. Selling things is his business and his fun. He has succeeded admirably in making his vocation his avocation. He would undoubtedly have made a success in any kind of merchandising enterprise that he had happened to fall into.

Nevertheless, his ability at holding together such a huge group as the Belk stores is fundamentally a matter of character—his own character. His large stockholding in some of the stores might give him the leverage to be a dictator; his own character is what has made him instead a somewhat patriarchal, thoroughly democratic leader. It is a temptation to speak of the Belk system as an empire and Mr. Belk as a mercantile empire builder. The word empire is completely inappropriate, and Mr. Belk is about as imperial as Benjamin Franklin.

And as in the case of Benjamin Franklin, Mr. Belk's merchandising philosophy takes the form of very simple maxims. "A bargain is a trade that leaves both the buyer and the seller feeling good." "A customer may not always be right, but a customer always has his rights." "Talking bad times always helps bring on bad times." "A one-trade customer won't help much. You've got to keep him coming back." "Honesty is the only policy." For Mr. Belk these are not just old sayings repeated without understanding—they are matters of faith, and through the Belk method of training young men for future responsibility as owner-managers, they have produced the operating methods that give a family character to the Belk stores. The Belk system is a perfect illustration of the saying that an institution is the lengthened shadow of a man.

Even today, a study would disclose that a majority of the heads of Belk stores have come from the farms of the Carolinas. Mr. Belk still believes that a farm boy offers the best prospects of success as a merchant. He is fond of quoting old Squire Hudson, the father of the Hudson brothers, that he raised two crops on his farm: first, cotton, and second, boys for the Belk Brothers.

"When a boy comes into town from a farm and starts working in a store," Mr. Belk will assert, with a wry smile, "he's used to long hours and hard work. At least, that used to be the case, anyway. He generally doesn't mind working. He's afraid that if he doesn't make good he'll have to go back to plowing."

That statement points to a fundamental characteristic of Henry Belk and the stores he heads. If in conversation with Mr. Belk you should refer to the Charlotte store as the "parent" store—meaning that it is the biggest store and the base of operations—he will check you sharply.

"No, Monroe is the parent store—that's where we got our start, Brother John and myself. We didn't plan it that way, but everything grew out of the Monroe store. And I'm still mighty interested in the Monroe store—and in Monroe too. I've got a lot of other investments down there."

And the truth is that the Monroe store is probably the typical Belk store—if there is any such thing. The expansion of the Belk group has avoided the South's big cities—Rich-

mond and Atlanta and Birmingham and Memphis and New
Orleans and Houston. And in most cases the stores even in
medium size cities like Charlotte and Greensboro and Winston-Salem were set up when the cities were much smaller and
have grown with the towns. These stores may bulk large in the
volume of sales, but the vast majority of the Belk stores are in
small cities or towns—places that combine a few small industries with a good rural trading area. They are places that
Henry Belk learned about when he was working in Monroe,
trying to be a success as a merchant and also trying to make
Monroe a balanced, prosperous community. In a way you
could say that the so-called Belk empire was nothing more
than Monroe and Union County, North Carolina, spread
across the map of the South, and that Henry Belk had made a
success without ever really leaving home.

VII

THE MAN

21

J OAB NELSON, UNCLE OF HENRY BELK'S GRANDFATHER, WAS
graduated from Yale. He returned to the Waxhaw section as
a teacher, and it is recorded that he "lifted that section of the
Waxhaws out of heathenism." The eulogy doubtless is overly
generous and the description of the locality libelous, for no
one man would have been capable of such improvement had
there been the occasion for it, nor is it likely that the Waxhaws, despite the presence in the community of such hardy
characters as Old Hickory Jackson, had ever sunk to such a
low estate.

But the description is indicative of the characters and abilities of many of the early settlers of the region, among whom were the Belks and the Walkups. The succeeding generations had been nourished out of devout Presbyterian stock, both of the regular and the Associate Reformed persuasions, and they testified to this nourishing in such individuals as the teacher, Joab Nelson. Thomas Milburn Belk was a member of the Associate Reformed Presbyterian denomination and was for many years an elder in the old Shiloh Church. His mother was a member of that church and perhaps his father, John Belk, Jr.

The Walkups were of staunch Scotch descent and were Presbyterians of the regular branch. Sarah Walkup Belk, singing psalms beside her husband in a church where hymns were forbidden as songs of worship in the House of God, longed for a closer affiliation with a regular Presbyterian church.

At length that time arrived. Henry Belk, looking back through the long decades, recalls his mother's return to the denomination of her upbringing.

"Old Tirzah Church was nearest to our house and we went there to church," he recalls. "It was an A.R.P. church. Well, a dispute arose in the church. I don't remember just what it was about, but it developed considerable heat, and the pastor, Dr. Robinson, decided that the thing to do was to turn over to the regular Presbyterian church, and about two-thirds of the members of old Tirzah went with him. So old Tirzah became a Presbyterian church, and it made my mother mighty happy."

It was from such deeply religious forebears that the Belk boys descended. They were reared in a household where the tenets of Presbyterians were strictly enjoined and upheld, where John Calvin and John Knox were household heroes along with Robert E. Lee and Stonewall Jackson. And yet, strangely, Henry Belk was twenty-one years old before he made his profession of faith in Jesus Christ and joined the church.

"There wasn't a Presbyterian church in Union County when we moved to Monroe while I was just a boy," Mr. Belk remembers. "There were mighty few Presbyterians living there —just a handful. But my mother wasn't going to let that be, so she started out to organize one."

Dr. D. A. Penick of Concord Presbytery organized a Sunday school, which the Belk boys attended, and a little later a church was established with seventeen charter members. But though young Henry attended the Sunday school and the services of the church, was being reared in a Christian home, and had come of a long line of strict Presbyterian forebears, he declined until long past childhood to affiliate with the church.

"I just didn't think I was good enough to join the church," he explained recently. "I felt that a fellow to be a member of the church ought to be a mighty good person and I just didn't think I was good enough.

"But when I was twenty-one years old and a grown man they had a revival in my mother's church and I was going to the services. The Reverend A. W. Miller, the pastor of the First Presbyterian Church of Charlotte and a wonderful preacher, was doing the preaching. One night he preached an unusually powerful sermon. I still remember it clearly. He was preaching on the text, 'God is love.' During the course of the sermon he went over some of the excuses that people make for staying out of the church. One of them was that you're not good enough. The preacher then went on to answer that argument.

" 'You say you are not good enough,' he said. 'The truth about the matter is that you are not good enough to stay out of the church. If you were perfect you wouldn't need to be in

the church. But you aren't perfect, you need the cleansing
blood of Jesus to make you fit to be a member of the church.
For that reason you should come to Him and be saved and
then you will be fit to join the church and strive to be a better
man or woman.'

"It sounded like a pretty good argument to me. It settled
the very point that had been bothering me all those years. I
went up to the preacher that night, confessed my sins and
accepted the Lord as my saviour, and joined the church. And
I have never regretted that step I took.

"There's much good in all churches, I think, and all of
them are headed in the same direction. But I just like the
Presbyterian brand best. It seems to me that Calvinism is the
best developer of sound Christian character. I believe that it
is likely, if a man follows it, to make him a strong, moral
force in his community. My mother was a strong Presbyterian
and I guess that has a lot to do with the way I feel about the
Presbyterian denomination."

His love for his denomination, as he indicates, is but another testimonial to the love he had for his mother and his
eagerness to testify to her greatness.

Having joined the church, young Belk characteristically
was unwilling to sit back and do little toward its operation
and support. With enthusiasm and as his developing business
permitted, he took a hand in the promotion of its work. During the period of 1892-1893 he and his brother employed the
Reverend Jonas Barclay as an evangelist in Union County.
It was the feeling of the two Belks and their mother that more
churches should be organized in the section. Christian work,
the Belks thought—and it is still the conviction of Henry
Belk—cannot go forward without churches. For that reason
he rarely, if ever, agrees to the wisdom of dissolving a church.
He does not hold with those who feel that there are too many
congregations, that fewer and larger churches would be more

effective in promoting the Christian religion's spread and influence.

"I think that there should be plenty of churches, even if some of them are small and weak," Mr. Belk declares. "There ought to be plenty of churches back in the country. If you wait until a fellow moves to town to get him to join a church, you won't likely have any success in getting him to join or show any interest if he does join. The country churches are the feeders for the big city churches. Many of the best church leaders come from the small country churches.

"And there should be plenty of churches in a city, too, churches that appeal to all sorts of people. If there are churches all over the city, churches whose members are rich and poor and high and low and the various stages in between, there'll be a church that will appeal to each and every fellow, where he'll be at home and won't feel uncomfortable. Big churches are good in their places, all right, but these big rich city churches just naturally won't reach all the people."

After the Reverend Mr. Barclay ended his work in Union County, the Reverend William Black, who was then beginning a long and highly successful career as an evangelist, was obtained as his successor. Then the Reverend R. J. McIlwaine was employed under the sponsorship of the Belk brothers to carry forward the work, and still later, the Reverend W. E. McIlwaine, D.D., his brother. Under the superintendency of the latter minister the one small Presbyterian church in Monroe grew into fifteen churches, and now there are more than twenty churches of that denomination in the county in which Mr. Belk's mother was instrumental in founding the first.

In the years that have followed, Mr. Belk's interest in the organization of Presbyterian churches has grown, and "outposts," as Mr. Belk calls those small organizations that have been established throughout the territory in which the Belks have opened their stores, have followed the stores in areas in which they had not already been established.

"I honestly believe that Mr. Belk gets more fun out of seeing a new Presbyterian church organized in a section where it has a chance of filling a very definite need than he does in seeing another Belk store started," an associate said one day. "Helping get Presbyterian churches organized and getting their church buildings and manses paid for—that is certainly one of his enthusiasms."

In the score of years during which Mr. Tyler has been associated with the Belk system of stores, he too has accumulated an interesting collection of anecdotes concerning the Charlotte merchant. One of these stories concerns Mr. Belk's well-known fondness for the Presbyterian denomination.

"One day Mr. Belk and I were traveling together to Elizabeth City," he said. "We were going through the little town of Hertford, down in eastern Carolina, when Mr. Henry saw an old Negro sitting on the curb on Main Street. He told his chauffeur to stop.

" 'Good morning, Uncle,' he said to the old fellow, when the car had stopped beside the old man. 'I wonder if you could tell me where the Presbyterian Church is?'

" 'What's dat?' the old Negro asked.

" 'The Presbyterian Church. Could you show us how to get to it?'

"The old darky shook his head slowly, as if in deep thought. Finally he spoke.

" 'Pres'terian Church—Pres'terians.' He shook his head again. 'No, suh,' he said, still shaking his grizzled head. 'No, suh, 'taint no sech peoples as dem anywhar 'round this here place.'

" 'Thank you, Uncle,' said Mr. Belk and he nodded to the chauffeur to drive on. The car moved off. Mr. Henry didn't say a word, nor did I. All the way to Elizabeth City neither of us mentioned it.

"And on another trip to Elizabeth City," Mr. Tyler added, "I had quite a bit of fun with Mr. Belk concerning our respective churches in that city. In fact, I think it resulted in the building of a fine new church there.

"I had always enjoyed joking with him about our church affiliations. Each of us always tried to outdo the other in upholding the honor of our respective denomination. It so happened that the Episcopal church had an unusually fine church plant and parish house in Elizabeth City. I was rather proud of this fact and I was anxious for Mr. Belk to see the church. In contrast, the Presbyterians were a small denomination in Elizabeth City and their church building at that time was a small, insignificant-looking frame building that seated only forty or fifty persons. Mr. Henry had never seen this little church.

"So one morning after we had arrived in Elizabeth City, I took him out to see the beautiful Episcopal church plant. He admired the handsome buildings and congratulated me on the progress my church had made there. Then he smiled broadly.

" 'Now let's go see the Presbyterian Church and I'll show you something.'

"So we went around to that little church, and when we got there his disappointment was quite evident. He looked at the little building a moment and smiled again.

" 'Now this church is all right,' he said, 'but I meant for us to go to the First Presbyterian Church. I wanted to see it.'

" 'This is it, Mr. Henry,' I said. 'This is the first, last, and only Presbyterian Church.'

"He didn't say any more about the church, and we went back to the store. But at the store he didn't get out of the car.

He just told me that he'd join me shortly, and he drove off. About two o'clock that afternoon he came back.

" 'Arthur,' he said, 'I've just bought a lot for a modern building for the Presbyterian church and the lot's right on Main Street.'

"Today a very handsome Presbyterian church stands on this beautiful lot in the very heart of the best residential section of Elizabeth City, a living memorial to the love Mr. Belk has for the church of his choice."

Although Henry Belk opened the Charlotte store in 1895 and moved his residence to that city from Monroe, he remained a member of the First Presbyterian Church of Monroe. Each Sunday he attended the services there and usually his mother accompanied him. He was an elder in the church and contributed generously to its support. He did not move his membership to Caldwell Memorial Presbyterian Church in Charlotte, which is located near his home and of which Mrs. Belk and the children were members, until after his mother's death in 1932.

He still contributes to the financial program of the church in Monroe, though the burden of his regular church contributions is now made through Caldwell Memorial.

The Belk philanthropies have centered in the main upon aid to churches, hospitals, and schools. One of the principal avenues of distribution has been the John M. Belk Memorial Fund, of which Karl G. Hudson is the trustee. Mr. Hudson, one of the Waxhaw "boys" of whom Mr. Belk is unusually proud, recently was reviewing the reasons for the establishment of the fund and its early operations.

"The late Dr. J. M. Belk and Mr. Henry Belk were always interested in home mission work," he declared. "They wanted especially to build churches in rural communities, and they encouraged the Synod's Home Missions committee to start a building fund. But it grew very slowly.

"About two weeks before his death on March 21, 1928, Dr. Belk was discussing the possibility of arranging for some of the stores each to contribute a hundred dollars every year to provide a base for such a building fund. He thought that such a plan would be an excellent way to assure a continuing support for the fund and that the encouragement it would give the Synod's committee in turn would cause that body to redouble its efforts to build up the fund.

"At a meeting of the store managers shortly after the death of Dr. Belk, it was proposed that a fund be set up to be known as the John M. Belk Memorial Fund and that it be set forth that the purpose of the fund would be the aiding of home mission churches. It was further proposed that each of the stores contribute a hundred dollars a year to this fund. Forty-two of the Belk stores contributed to the establishment of this fund and Mr. Belk has encouraged the stores each year since that time to contribute."

Mr. Hudson modestly failed to mention that he was the man who made the original proposals to establish this fund as a memorial to Dr. Belk. But he was, and his leadership in the movement was promptly recognized. He has been the trustee and key figure in its development and management from the beginning.

More than 335 churches and manses have already been assisted in their building operations with money provided by the memorial fund, and the great majority of these programs has been carried out in home mission fields. In many instances the programs would never have been successful had it not been for the fund's assistance, and very likely others would never have been attempted.

These churches and homes of pastors and their families are scattered throughout the general area in which Belk stores are located—in North Carolina, South Carolina, Virginia, Tennessee, Georgia, Alabama, Mississippi, and Florida.

Henry Belk became a member of the North Carolina Synod's Home Missions committee in 1905 and has been a member of the committee continuously since that date. He has contributed largely to the support of the committee's activities, but his gifts made independently of the committee and of the J. M. Belk Memorial Fund have been larger. He supports home missionaries in several areas and provides substantial aid also in the work of the church in foreign fields. Through the Synod's Church and Manse Erection League, formed many years ago, he has helped build scores of churches and manses within the area of the Synod's work.

It has always been Henry Belk's policy to help finance rather than finance completely any church project, and his usual method is to provide the brick for the structure.

"That gives them a good start on their building and it insures a permanent type of structure, too," Mr. Belk explains. "I don't believe in doing too much for a fellow or for a congregation. If you go ahead and do it all, then the man—or the congregation, as it may be—doesn't have as much interest in the thing as he would have had if he had done part of the work or got up some of the money."

The Belk philanthropies, however, are not restricted to Presbyterian churches. Many Belk dollars have gone to projects related to the denomination in the fields of education and medical care. He has given largely to the program at Montreat, the Presbyterian summer colony in the mountains of western North Carolina, where years ago he built a large home in which he spends several weeks each summer. He had a large part in the building of the new seven-story Presbyterian hospital in Charlotte, which occupies a large wooded tract beside his own home on Hawthorne Lane, an institution that he had aided generously when years ago it was taken over

BELK-BEERY COMPANY, Wilmington, North Carolina

BELK-LOGAN COMPANY, Forest City, North Carolina

BELK'S DEPARTMENT STORE, Union, South Carolina

GALLANT-BELK COMPANY, Athens, Georgia

by his denomination and has continued to aid in the years it has been operating.

It would be impossible to compile a list of all those institutions that have been aided by Belk money. One, however, in which he has been interested particularly and to which he has contributed heavily is Presbyterian Junior College at Maxton, North Carolina. For many years he has been a trustee of the college. He has watched through the years the results of its work and has participated in the formation and carrying forward of its program.

The Charlotte merchant, in fact, is a trustee of a large number of institutions and organizations of an educational and philanthropical nature, including Davidson College, the Montreat Retreat Association, the Presbyterian hospital in Charlotte, and various boards and commissions within the framework of the Presbyterian church in the South. For many years he was a trustee of the Presbyterian Orphans' Home at Barium Springs in Iredell County, North Carolina. This home, where for many years hundreds of boys and girls have been reared to become honored and effective citizens of their various communities, has always held one of the warmest places in Mr. Belk's affection, for he has never forgotten his own orphaned childhood in the despairing days of the Reconstruction.

The Belks have not been interested within their church work in home missions alone, however, nor in church-related educational institutions within the home areas, even though more emphasis has been placed upon their support of these home programs. One venture in the foreign field, started many years ago by the two brothers, continues to hold a primary position in the surviving brother's affections. It is the Sarah Walkup Hospital in Tai-chow, China. The hospital was opened in July, 1922, and its establishment marked the beginning of the medical work of the Presbyterian church in

Tai-chow, one of the largest mission points in the great North Kiang-su mission.

A large hospital plant and excellently equipped, it has been of invaluable service to thousands of Chinese. During World War II, when for a time the Japanese conquerors occupied the area just north of the Yangtse River near which it is located, the hospital was looted of much of its equipment, but the buildings were little harmed and it is now reported to be functioning normally. Over a long period of its service the hospital was operated under the management of Dr. R. B. Price, known to most Presbyterians acquainted with foreign mission activities as one of the great mission leaders in the Orient.

After providing the plant, the Belks have contributed regularly to the support of the institution, and since Dr. Belk's death his brother has continued an affectionate interest in its work and has given material aid toward its support. Mrs. Simpson, too, until the very end of her life, was a frequent contributor to the program of the hospital. She sent a veritable wealth of gifts to the members of the staff and the patients. She was especially proud of the institution which her sons had named in her honor.

A great many of Mr. Belk's gifts have been contributed either anonymously or to persons who appreciated but did not publicly acclaim their receipt.

"Henry Belk has done a lot of good that mighty few people know about," his long-time friend, former Governor and Senator Cameron Morrison said of him one day. "He never liked to make a fuss about anything and especially about his gifts to people. There's many a fellow who's been helped by Henry Belk, and Dr. John Belk, too, and no one except he and the Belks ever knew what went on between them. They were always helping folks, and Mr. Belk still is. A mighty little of the good he does gets in the newspapers."

To honor Mr. Belk and memorialize his long interest in the church, his associates in the Gallant-Belk group of stores sponsored the building of a handsome church structure in the Homeland Park section of Anderson, South Carolina, at a cost of about seventy thousand dollars. The Gallant-Belk group contributed fifty thousand and the First Presbyterian Church of Anderson and the citizens of Homeland Park provided the remaining amount. The Henry Belk Presbyterian Church, which seats two hundred and fifty people, bears in a prominent position this inscription on a bronze tablet:

ERECTED 1948—1949
TO THE GLORY OF GOD
AND TO HONOR A GREAT CHRISTIAN
LAYMAN AND BUSINESS MAN
WILLIAM HENRY BELK

A similar tribute is the beautiful Belk chapel being erected on the campus of Queens College—an institution to which he has contributed generously—as a memorial to William Henry Belk and the late Dr. John M. Belk. This towering structure, which is to occupy a commanding site on the completed Queens campus, was contributed to the college by the managers of the Belk stores in memory of the founders. No other form of memorial could please Mr. Belk more.

One of the greatest Belk contributions, and one that is likely to be of great practical use down through the years, was announced in 1949 at the opening dinner of the Davidson College Development Program's campaign for $2,500,000 with which to enlarge its endowment fund and greatly increase its physical facilities.

"It is my privilege to announce that the Belk family and business associates," said Irwin Belk, one of the sons of the merchant, "are making plans to sponsor the project for a new dormitory at Davidson College to be known as W. H. Belk Hall, and are actively seeking the favorable consideration of the several Belk store corporations in the furtherance of this needed addition to the campus." The gift, estimated at not less than $300,000, was by far the largest single contribution to the development program campaign and one of the greatest benevolences recorded in the South during the year.

22

Mr. and mrs. Belk have six children, three married, and one grandson. All six children are actively interested in the operation of the Belk stores.

One day as Mr. Belk was talking of his family he pointed above his desk to the framed portraits of the six children.

"I have six," he said. "But if I had got married at the usual time folks marry, I guess I'd had twice that many or more. I always said I wanted the same size family old Jacob in the Bible had—twelve sons and two daughters. I didn't do quite half as well as Jacob, but I guess I was a lot later starting."

Mr. Belk chuckled.

"I like large families. My grandfather had a large one, about the right size, I figure. But I guess I was just too busy getting my business started and going successfully to give much thought then to getting married."

After their marriage the Belks settled down to keeping house. For Henry Belk the experience of again living in a house after the long years of living in an apartment above the store was rather novel. It was his second residence in Charlotte, and he would have but two others. The Belks are not given to moving about. The house was at 804 North Tryon Street, not far from the home of Mrs. Belk's parents. It was down near the end of the street in that day and close to the Seaboard passenger station.

When Henry Belk married in June of 1915, his brother had been married almost twenty-six years. The Charlotte merchant had spent many happy week ends in Monroe with John Belk's family of seven daughters.

"Brother John had a family of fine girls," Mr. Belk said recently in reminiscing. "And by the time I got married they were pretty well grown up, the most of them, and they liked to put on a lot of style, which was all right.

"Well, one day after we had settled down pretty well at keeping house out on North Tryon Street, my cook Adeline came to me and said she'd like to have a word with me. We had brought Adeline up from Monroe. She knew all Brother John's folks, of course, and how they ran their house down there.

" 'Mr. Belk,' Adeline said to me, 'we ought to have a butler.'

" 'A butler!' I said. 'Why do you think we ought to have a butler, Adeline?' I asked her. 'You don't have much to do, just cooking for Mrs. Belk and me and yourself, just the three of us. How come you think we should get a butler?'

" 'Well, Mr. Belk,' she answered, 'we just ought to have a butler. Dr. John's got one.'

" 'But, Adeline,' I said to her, 'they're rich folks down in Monroe. We just have to struggle along and do the best we can.' "

Mr. Belk hastened to explain that he was intending no criticism of his brother's family—that he had merely been teasing the cook. "Brother John and I always got along fine. Whatever he did suited me and whatever I did generally suited him too. Anyway he acted like it did, and I think it did."

The year after his marriage—on June 29, 1916—Mr. Belk had business at the old Presbyterian Hospital, which at that time was on the corner of West Trade and Mint Streets, across from the post office.

"I wasn't able to give anybody much help that day," he said, in recalling that momentous occasion. "I reckon I just got in the way. That was the day Henry was born." When Henry was still a baby they moved from the house on North Tryon Street.

At this time, the Elizabeth College property on Hawthorne Lane was to be sold, since the college had been having difficult times financially and it had been determined to suspend operations. The college occupied the southern part of a beautifully wooded tract on Hawthorne Lane and Caswell Road between East Fourth and East Fifth Streets at the head of Elizabeth Avenue.

When this property was made available for purchase, the Presbyterians bought the college buildings and about fifteen acres of the twenty-five acre tract, and for fifty thousand dollars Mr. Belk purchased the remainder of the tract. He helped provide the funds with which the college property was purchased for the hospital and indorsed a note with which the remaining amount needed was procured.

The Belks moved into the old residence that fronted toward the hospital on Hawthorne Lane at the northern end of the tract and the Presbyterians converted the college into a hospital.

"One day quite awhile after we had moved out to Hawthorne Lane I saw Bob Dunn," Mr. Belk recalled. "Bob was a cousin of mine; in fact, Bob's mother was my first cousin. He had been brought up a mighty poor boy, but Bob was always a fine fellow and a hard worker and by now he was a rich man. He was president of the Commercial Bank in Charlotte, and he owned a lot of property.

" 'Henry,' Bob said to me that day, 'you've got a mighty fine tract out there where you are living. It's a beautiful place. But that house doesn't go with the tract. What you ought to do is put you up a fine residence out there.'

" 'Bob,' I said, 'I'd like to have a real nice house, but where'd I get the money to build it with?'

" 'From me,' Bob said. 'You get the plans drawn up and I'll let you have the money.'

" 'Bob,' I said, 'I just might take you up on that offer.'

" 'Well, I mean it,' said Bob. 'You ought to build yourself a fine house out there on that nice property.'

"Well, we moved the old house we were living in back to front on Caswell Road at the rear of the property, and I built the house we're living in now. The other house is a pretty nice house. We have been renting it ever since. I had the new house put in Mary's name. It's her property. She just lets me stay out there. I've been living there a pretty good while. I guess she won't run me off after all these years." Mr. Belk paused, grinned. "But I'll tell you one thing. She certainly could if she wanted to. It's her property, all right."

Mrs. Henry Belk agrees that the house is hers, but in a rather different fashion. "Mr. Belk told me soon after we were married that he'd make me a proposition—he would turn the house over to me entirely and I should run it as I thought best if I would agree to let him run the store in the same way. Well, he has certainly not concerned himself with the house. If he hadn't let me run it, it just wouldn't have been run. I'll bet he hasn't bought groceries a dozen times since we've been married. He would be horrified if he knew how high things to eat are now. Several years ago he went with me to the grocery and he couldn't get over the fact that bacon cost forty-five cents a pound. He said if it went any higher he would just have to stop eating bacon. I wonder sometimes what he would say if he knew the bacon he was eating was nearly a dollar a pound."

Although Henry Belk has always spent long and hard hours at the store and never interfered with the running of the house, he has enjoyed his home tremendously and has always liked to be at home. Mrs. Belk says that it is the hardest thing in the world to get him to go anywhere at night, he is happiest just being at home.

The Belks have indeed had a singularly happy home life. Until their son Irwin's marriage in August, 1948, all six of the children had lived with their parents. Henderson, next to the youngest, married in the summer of 1949. Henry, Jr., was married in January, 1950. The Belks are a closely knit group in their business activities, too, and the six children continue taking over many of the functions of operating the great Belk merchandising organization. And always for their father and mother the six children maintain and show the warmest affection and admiration.

"My father is always asking us what we should do about such and such a problem," his son John said one day in discussing Mr. Belk's interest in training the younger Belks in the ways of modern merchandising. "He is turning over to us much of the routine operation of the Belk organization. But don't misunderstand me. My father's still very much the head man around Belk Brothers Company and the buying office. And he still knows what he's doing and just how to get it done. If I do say so, my father's a very remarkable man."

Mr. Belk enjoys having his family around him, and often during the summer months he likes to slip away to some old church yard down in the Waxhaw country for a family reunion and picnic. Christmas holidays and birthday anniversaries he welcomes, too, with all the delight of a small child.

All of Mr. Belk's sons entered Davidson College as freshmen, although John was the only one to be graduated from that institution. Henry Belk, Jr., is a Duke University graduate, Sarah finished at Sweet Briar in Virginia, Irwin and Tom are graduates of the University of North Carolina, and Henderson earned his diploma from Duke. Few families have had as many sons in the service during the war as the Henry Belks. All five boys served, John and Irwin in the army and Henry, Henderson, and Tom in the navy.

Mrs. Belk's interests outside her home and church have centered in the main upon the various programs of the Daughters of the American Revolution. She has served in many high posts in that patriotic society, including those of regent of the North Carolina chapters and chaplain general of the national organization. Mrs. Belk has also taken much interest in the programs and activities of the Colonial Dames.

A recent enthusiasm of Mrs. Belk has been the promotion of the plan to restore the historic Hezekiah Alexander Rock House six miles from Charlotte. This house, the only remaining structure in the county dating back to Revolutionary times, was built in 1774 by Hezekiah Alexander, a signer of the Mecklenburg Declaration of Independence and brother of Mrs. Belk's ancestor of that day, John McKnitt Alexander.

Mr. Belk expressed characteristically his wife's interest in things historical:

"Mary has always liked to look up old history. She goes to a lot of D. A. R. meetings and suchlike. Right now she and several of the other ladies are mighty interested in fixing up the old Alexander Rock House. She's descended from the Alexanders, you know. In fact, Mary's kin to about everybody in the county whose folks have been here a long time. Not long after we married I said to Mary one day:

" 'Mary,' I said, 'the only trouble about being married to you is that I can't cuss out a soul in this whole country round here without being scared that I'm cussing out some of your kinfolks, and that just wouldn't do!' "

The Belks are an average American family in many respects.

"We have always sought to teach the children responsibility, and we have probably bent over backwards in trying to keep from spoiling them," Mrs. Belk says. "I suspect that Mr. Belk and I in many cases have been too strict with the children and haven't allowed them as much spending money as we should have. They have worked as children for very small earnings and they have never been brought up as rich children—rich in the sense that you commonly understand the word to mean. I suspect that our children would probably have had more if they had been in poorer circumstances. We were always so afraid that we would spoil them. But they are good children, if I do say it, and unspoiled. We're mighty proud of them."

And they are very proud of their new daughters, too. Irwin, the first to marry, the fourth child of the Belks, married Miss Carol Grotnes, daughter of Mr. and Mrs. Charles G. Grotnes of Ridge Park, Illinois, and Henderson, their fifth child, married Miss Ann Everett, daughter of Mr. and Mrs. H. H. Everett of Charlotte. Henry, Jr., married Miss Phyllis Harper, another Charlotte girl, daughter of the Floyd I. Harpers.

About the remaining member of the Belk family they are enthusiastic. Mr. Belk, beaming more happily than if he had just opened a big new store, held the silver urn when the Irwin Belks stood up to have their son baptized.

23

T HE VISITING NEWSPAPERMAN SAT IN A CUSHIONY LEATHER chair facing the great walnut desk in the Belk Buying Service building's big corner office. As he listened to the tall, spare man talk, he wiggled the sole of his right shoe in the luxuriously thick green carpet.

"Mr. Belk," the newspaperman said, when the merchant paused, "when you were a young man just starting out down there at Monroe, did you ever figure that some time you'd have a swanky office like this—indirect lighting, walnut-paneled walls, leather chairs, ankle-deep carpet—" he swept his arm in an embracing arc—"all this luxury?"

The tall man chuckled and looked across the room, circled with the framed photographs of scores of the Belk stores, toward the picture of the original store at Monroe.

"No," he said, "I don't guess I did. I was too busy getting my business started to be thinking about what sort of office I'd have sometime. I was interested in selling goods." He settled back in his chair and faced his interviewer, an expression almost apologetic on his face.

"This is a nice office, isn't it?" he said. "I didn't see any need for such a fine office for me—wasn't used to such finery. But, as I believe I told you before, Sarah and the boys thought that they'd like to fix me up a nice one in the new building and I told them just to go ahead and fix it the way they wanted to, that whatever they did would suit me fine. It is a pretty big jump from that old office I had down at Monroe—just a little partitioned-off place made pretty much out of drygoods boxes. And it's nicer than the one over at the store, too. I thought that was a mighty fine office—certainly good enough for me." He chuckled again. "But like I said, Sarah and the boys wanted to fix up this one, and I told them to go right ahead." His eyes peeped out slyly above the rims of his glasses. "I don't have to stay in here all the time anyway."

His interviewer laughed and suddenly was serious again.

"Mr. Belk," said he, "I saw in a magazine the other day —some trade magazine, I think it was—where some writer described you as the greatest merchant, in his opinion, in the world. Certainly many people considered the Belk organization the most unusual merchandising enterprise in the world. You've had wonderful success. It must make you mighty proud to realize how your business has grown, doesn't it?"

Mr. Belk considered a moment.

"Well, yes, it does. I guess I'll have to admit. I started out pretty much from scratch. But we still make plenty of mistakes. We lose money some times. We aren't always right."

The reporter pursued his theme.

"And you have been able to do a lot of mighty fine things with your money. It must be satisfying. As a newspaperman, of course, I wouldn't know anything about that."

"Well, now—" Mr. Belk's sharp eyes narrowed. "Sometimes I have to turn people down that I don't like to. Had a delegation in here today wanting a large contribution from me. They had a good cause, too, a mighty good cause. And I did give them something, but not as much as they wanted me to. I just don't have the money to do what I'd like to and what a lot of folks expect me to.

"A lot of money comes in, of course, but a lot goes out, too, a mighty lot of it. Taxes. They eat you up. And instead of coming down, they're always going up. Seems like the government just doesn't know how to cut expenses. If a man makes any money nowadays, he can't keep it; he can't even put much of it back into the business, and he's afraid to try to do much expanding."

He paused, leaned forward, his face grave.

"Yes, sir," he said, "a lot goes for taxes. And a man's got to support his family on what's left."

He swiveled his big chair around to face his desk, a roller-top model identical with the one in his office on the fourth floor of the Charlotte store, and glanced at the weekly summary of the stores' business. Then he looked up again.

"A lot of folks aren't anything like as rich as some folks think they are," he declared. "In fact, after the taxes come out, you just can't have much left."

"I believe in progress," he hastened to add, "and I like to see the country moving forward. I'm not one to stand back and insist on old ways of doing things. I like progress. But I don't believe the way we're going now is progress. I believe we're heading the wrong way. You can't tax a country into prosperity. There's too many people depending upon the government to take care of them. Folks are losing their old spirit of dare, of trying to get ahead, and are talking nowadays all the time about security. You've got to work if you want to get anywhere, nowadays just the same as it was when I was a boy. You've got to produce. There's too big a number riding on the backs of the rest. And now, when things are prosperous, is the time for us to be paying off our debts—the government, I mean. But instead of that we're spending more and more and up in Washington they seem to figure that the only solution is more taxes. It's bad business."

Staunchly southern, born and reared in the very air that gave Andrew Jackson to the Democratic party, brought up in the bitter days of Reconstruction and suspicious of most things northern, including the Republican party of a few years back, Mr. Belk might reasonably be expected to be a Democrat. He is perhaps a Jeffersonian Democrat, as his statement concerning taxes would indicate. He supports the ticket of his party in local and state elections, though in the years since the advent of the New Deal and its child the Fair Deal he has frequently had grievous doubts. He denied that he has deserted the Democratic faith; the Democratic household, he contends and many others likewise, has deserted the ancient faith, to go out in search of strange and politically unorthodox gods. Anything that smacks of the unorthodox is anathema to Henry Belk. He looks back through the years to a religious faith and a political system blessed and nourished by the fathers.

Like many of the great business leaders of a generation which has disappeared or is fast disappearing, Mr. Belk looks with horror upon any political system resembling what frequently is termed, for lack of a better description, "the welfare state." He contemplates this nation as still the land

W. H. BELK HALL, Davidson College

BELK'S CHAPEL, Queen's College

W. H. BELK and W. E. GALLANT, manager of the Anderson, South Carolina, store

of opportunity, a country in which initiative and energy can count for much, one of the few remaining areas of earth where a poor country boy willing to work and use his brains might even yet become a great business leader with millions of dollars to command as he feels they could serve best.

He belongs with the age of James Buchanan Duke, who was for years a Charlotte resident and whom he much admired, Charles M. Schwab, Henry Ford, Harvey Firestone, Filene, the father of today's Cannons, and others of that era of great national development whose names are synonymous with the advance of American industry. He belongs with that age, yet in many respects he was not of it. For many men of that period, the last half century and even in the years before, were ruthless men, caring nothing for their fellowmen as such, looking upon them simply as pawns to be moved in the game of making money and more money, as cogs in the faster and faster turning wheels of American industry. Mr. Belk was not and has never been in any sense a ruthless man. There is nothing about him that would tend to qualify him as one of the "robber barons."

But though Henry Belk has little patience with certain modern political doctrines, particularly that of deficit spending by the government, he is distinctly a modernist in his business thinking. Although his roots run out far into the remote past years, and though his patron saints are John Calvin and Robert E. Lee—and which of the two holds first place in his affections he himself perhaps does not know—he is as modern in his business approach to problems of today as the concrete, tile, and chromium building over which he holds dominion as head of the gigantic Belk mercantile empire.

Nothing ventured, nothing gained, has been his motto through the long years. He is always willing to take a chance —with a business proposition or a business man—provided he can see a reasonable prospect of success. That is one reason why he is so alarmed when heavy taxes deprive industry of venture capital.

"In times of depression when most people were blue and pessimistic and almost ready to give up," said one of Mr. Belk's associates recently, "he was looking ahead, confident that things would soon be on the mend and that good times would be back, bringing even greater prosperity. In such times as that he has perhaps best demonstrated his business ability. He has kept right along with his job of selling goods and at the same time he was keeping his eyes and ears open. He has always been willing to bet on his city, his county, his state, and the nation generally. He's had some tough going at times, of course—who hasn't?—but I've never seen him when he wasn't confident that eventually conditions would be good again, and he's kept right on going with the assurance that the future held promise of even better things."

A stranger to the Belk family would never suspect that William Henry Belk was eighty-seven years old on June 2, 1949. Tall, lean—like his boys—he still has abundant good health, great physical vitality for a man of his age, and a lively zest for living. Certainly no one could say that his mental capacities show deterioration with the years. He comes regularly to the office, keeps sharply abreast of everything that is developing in the fast expanding stores' organization, and takes an active interest in the current scene—economically, politically, socially. In addition to this, his interest in the affairs of the church has in no way lessened.

"Some folks have asked me if I ever expect to retire," he said one day recently. Then he turned his sharp eyes upon his visitor, as if the latter had made the suggestion. "What would I want to retire for?" he asked, challengingly. "I'm not overworked, I guess. I like to stay busy. You know, I still like to sell things. I reckon I will as long as I live." Mr.

Belk has often expressed the hope that he may live as long as his mother did. She lived to be almost ninety-six.

Mr. Belk's associates and members of the family are convinced that the Charlotte merchant's forward look, his eagerness for initiating new enterprises and seeing them advance successfully from the start, coupled with his daily zest for living have been responsible in large part for his excellent health and maintained vigor.

Customers of the Charlotte store are not altogether surprised when they find themselves occasionally being waited on by the head man of the great Belk empire.

He also enjoys sitting in his office and talking with friends —old friends from Monroe and the Waxhaw country and the many other communities in which the older Belk stores are located. He knows countless persons—Presbyterian preachers, returned missionaries, the younger friends and associates of his children, merchants in competing department stores, political leaders, and figures in the field of education. Yet Mr. Belk never gives audiences. He could not be formal; he simply sits and talks. He talks the language of the ordinary mortal, whether he is talking with a college president, the chairman of the board of a great business corporation, or one of the youngest clerks in the basement department of the Charlotte store.

It is amazing to his associates in the Belk's Buying Service office how well Mr. Belk keeps informed of the business being done by the widely separated stores. He knows what each store is doing, how its business this week compared with the business done the week before. He can tell you what the smallest store is doing, how its operation costs are related to its profits, the amount of capitalization, the volume of business done in any given period, and the amount of stock on its shelves.

"It really is remarkable how well Mr. Belk keeps informed

on the condition of business throughout the great Belk system of stores," Mr. Anderson, the controller, will invariably observe when someone mentions Mr. Belk's ability at keeping abreast of merchandising conditions. "He gets weekly reports from the stores, of course, and he studies these reports carefully. He makes little scribbled hieroglyphics on the margins of these sheets, little penciled notations that nobody else can understand, and he can tell you any time exactly what the situation is in any store in the nearly three hundred of the Belk organization."

Mr. Belk still enjoys opening new stores. A store to him is an adventure, a challenge, a frontier. Frequently he travels hundreds of miles to attend the formal opening of a new Belk store. His smile and his merry eyes demonstrate at each of these functions that he is as pleased as the young manager who envisions himself starting upon a journey that may even parallel the Belk story itself.

He is no joiner, except of the church, the Scottish and York Rite Masons, and the Order of the Mystic Shrine. His sons and most of his executives are also members of these groups. When he leaves his office he goes home, and only once in a great while does he go out at night. He goes to church regularly and frequently attends meetings of various church bodies. Occasionally he goes out to some social function or a show of some sort—"entertainment," he describes it.

But after three-quarters of a century his greatest entertainment is the daily routine of going to work. But he is not yet altogether and completely comfortable in his handsome new office, whose beautiful furnishings and paneled walls speak success. It represents for Henry Belk the heights which he has attained. But Mr. Henry—as he is called by virtually everyone in the great Belk establishment who knows him, and few do not—is not particularly interested in the heights. He would rather be out on the sales floor where the clerks are selling goods. A visitor can never be sure that he will find Mr. Belk in that fine new office in the Belk's Buying Service building during office hours. He might find him instead at the store, in the piece goods department, perhaps, or down in the basement, for the basement is the place to which the folks eventually come, especially the folks in from the country. Or Mr. Belk might be found in the Belk Bargain Store on North College Street. And it is quite possible if the visitor did find Mr. Belk there and asked him for two or three yards of cloth, the head man of the southeast's greatest merchandising organization would pull his little scissors out of his vest pocket and snip it off.

For to Henry Belk selling goods was always his greatest sport.

VIII

LAST YEARS

24

NOR DID MR. BELK EVER LOSE HIS ZEST FOR SELLING.
From boyhood he had been going regularly to the store.
Buying and selling had been his vocation and his avocation,
his business and his pleasure. He had never had time, or
taken it, for sports, either as a participant or spectator, and
never for a moment had he entertained the thought of retiring from business. He enjoyed the very scent of quality
merchandise freshly unpacked and shelved and stacked, the
shuffle of customers meandering past the counters, the small
talk of the clerks and the people being waited on. He liked

that much better, in fact, than the formal elegance of his great walnut-paneled office in the Belk Buying Service building a few doors from the East Fifth Street entrance of the huge Belk Brothers store.

"This is a nice place, all right," he would agree as he swiveled around from his big desk, and his merry eyes would sparkle in his otherwise sober face, "but I like it better over there at the store. Over there they're taking in money; over here we're paying it out."

In the Belk Buying Service office, of course, they were taking in money too, often in big checks, but it lacked the atmosphere of selling, and Mr. Belk's plush and proper office did not have about it the smell of drygoods displayed and the onrush of eager customers. Often the head of the great and growing Belk merchandising domain would slip quietly from his office up the street to the store, and sometimes he would sell to a customer in the basement a few yards from a bolt of figured cloth. Now and then he would also visit the College Street store where cheaper prices prevailed. He wanted to keep his hand in the selling. He still liked the feel of it.

Henry Belk could not abide laziness. He taught his boys to work and work hard. Despite his great wealth and his many years, he never permitted himself to retire to the rocking chair and the soft slippers. As long as he was able he came regularly to his office, and while he was there he was busy. He continued an active oversight of the now fast growing business of the more than three hundred Belk stores. He continued to study the stores' regular reports of business done, and beside the figures in the long columns he continued to scrawl his penciled hieroglyphics that only he could decipher. His counsel was sought and followed; his instructions were carried out to the letter. Henry Belk to the end of his days was head man in his spreading great empire.

One of the things he continued to enjoy in the hours spent in his Buying Service office was meeting his friends—men and women in many and widely varying fields. He liked people; he never did want to get far away from them nor be away from them long.

"Henry Belk had good country raisin'," a friend through many years observed of him one day, "and he never did get away from it."

A man's position in life, the potentialities of his checkbook, seemed to have little effect upon Henry Belk's opinion of him. He often had in his office leaders of his denomination—preachers, officers of the presbytery, the synod, and the Presbyterian General Assembly; returned missionaries home on furlough; college presidents; and also unlettered humble parishioners, white and Negro, seeking aid for their little churches or for church-related causes of one kind and another. He treated them all with uniform kindness and consideration.

Frequently in his long years there had come to his office a procession of men and women in politics seeking his advice, his contributions to their campaigns, his influence in helping them win votes. Perhaps few men never active in politics had more friends and acquaintances among the politicians than Mr. Belk, and he treated a candidate for constable with the same courtesy he showed a candidate for United States Senate. Doubtless it was good business, for constables' families were good Belk customers, but it was also Mr. Belk's inherent way.

Often, too, the Charlotte merchant was visited by leaders of the nation's industry. One day in February before his eighty-eighth birthday he proudly introduced to a Charlotte newspaper reporter a guest he and Mrs. Belk were entertaining in their home.

"I've been hearing and reading about this young man a

long time, and I've always admired him," he said. "But this is the first opportunity I've had of knowing him personally and getting his views. And after talking with him a good deal I think I can say that we've got pretty much the same ideas about things."

The "young man" was J. C. Penney, the Missouri-born merchant who the following September would be seventy-five. The Charlotte merchant enjoyed Mr. Penney's visit. They talked about many things and were in agreement on most. One of the points of accord was each one's love of selling. Mr. Belk's family of stores at that time exceeded 300; Mr. Penney's chain had 1609. The two merchants quickly recognized the fact that they had traveled remarkably parallel courses in their journeying to great affluence. Seated before Mr. Belk's big roll-top desk, the visiting merchant traced the similarity of their careers.

"It's amazing how Mr. Belk's life and mine parallel each other," he remarked. "Each of us started from scratch; his folks were poor and mine were poor. Both of us started off clerking in stores. Mr. Belk says he got five dollars a month, but when I came along a few years later they'd upped wages considerably; I got $2.27 a week."

The two agreed that hard work is usually the foundation of success.

"Yes, hard work's necessary," Mr. Penney declared. "Industry, which is hard work, and character are the qualities that will carry a young man to the top. But he must have character as his foremost asset if he's to be successful. Adaptation to his line of work is very important and he must apply himself diligently and pursue his line of work relentlessly. But character is the essential thing."

They congratulated each other on another parallel. Each was the subject of a new biography. *Main Street Merchant*, the story of Mr. Penney's career, was then having wide distribution, and a few months later—on Friday, June 2—the Belk biography, published by The University of North Carolina Press, would commemorate Henry Belk's eighty-eighth birthday anniversary.

The week his book came out brought other honors to the Charlotte merchant. On Sunday, June 4, the handsome Belk chapel on the campus of Queens College in Charlotte, a gift to the institution by the families and associates of Mr. Belk and the late Dr. John M. Belk, was used for the first time when the baccalaureate sermon of the 1950 commencement was preached from its pulpit by Dr. Julian Lake, pastor of the First Presbyterian Church of Winston-Salem, North Carolina. That afternoon the chapel was formally dedicated and the cornerstone set. Among the several articles placed in the cornerstone was a copy of the Belk biography.

Twenty miles away at Davidson College the next day, William Henry Belk, the Waxhaws country boy, stood on the rostrum in cap and gown and in the formal hush of traditional academism heard President John R. Cunningham confer upon him an honorary doctorate.

"William Henry Belk," Dr. Cunningham read the citation that preceded the hooding, "president of a great business; director of various important corporations; staunch supporter of the program of Home Missions and Church Extension in your Presbytery and Synod; patron, trustee, and benefactor of David College; beloved and inspiring father— Davidson College is happy to confer upon you the honorary degree of Doctor of Laws."

Henry Belk sat down to the applause of the approving great audience. A few minutes later he marched out in the academic recession, and as it broke up he handed his citation and diploma to his wife; he returned at once to the robing room to leave the borrowed cap and doctor's gown; that evening the new hood of gay stripes hung in his bedroom

closet never to be worn again; in fact, in all probability
Henry Belk never again laid eyes on any of the trappings of
his moment of academic glory, though he appreciated greatly
Davidson College's honoring him.

The next morning he was back in his office. The week had
been perhaps one of the most exciting of his later years.
Publication of his book had pleased Mr. Belk immensely. "I
don't see why anybody'd write a book about me," he modestly
told many a friend as he presented an autographed copy,
"but I do appreciate it."

Mr. Belk must have autographed scores of the books. He
kept them stacked in one of the cabinets near his desk and
he gave them out generously. Sometimes he would mention
the name of a friend in some distant city and ask his secretary to see that a book was mailed to him.

He enjoyed the congratulatory letters from friends and the
reviews of the book. For many years he had been reading
newspaper stories of his business ventures, as well as his
activities in behalf of churches and other philanthropies. He
had been the subject of many a feature article, but now
he was on book pages; carefully and with evident enjoyment
he read the clippings sent him by the newspapers' literary edi-
tors, Belk store managers, and other friends.

His greatest satisfaction in these years beyond eighty,
however, he confided to his more intimate friends, was the
fact that his children were marrying and establishing homes
of their own.

"A man ought to get married while he's young—before
he's too old to get set in his ways," he would suggest. "I
guess I should have married when I was younger. I would
have had a longer time to enjoy married life. There's nothing as satisfying as having a good home and a nice family.
I was so busy getting my business going, I guess, that I just
didn't take time to start courting when I should have. As it

is, I'm old enough to be my children's grandfather and consequently I can't expect to be with them," he would reiterate, "so many more years, though my forebears were long-lived folks and my mother lived to be past ninety-five."

He did not live as long as his mother had lived, but he did live long enough to see three of his sons married and to be best man in each one's wedding. He lived to hold four grandchildren in his arms. The three daughters-in-law and the first grandchild came into the family in time to be included in the Belk biography. Two other grandchildren were born soon after the book was published: Irene Grotnes, daughter of Mr. and Mrs. Irwin Belk, on June 28, and Tommy Everett, son of Mr. and Mrs. Henderson Belk, on August 25. The next year, on October 27, 1951, Mary Henry, the first child of Mr. and Mrs. William Henry Belk, Jr., was born. Nothing delighted Mr. Belk more than to learn that a new heir was expected in any of the three families.

During this period the Belk family of stores was also adding members in many of the southeastern states. Mr. Belk participated in the formal openings of several of the new stores, even though it required long travel for a man nearing ninety, for he enjoyed no occasion more than that of the launching of a new Belk enterprise, except perhaps the dedication of a new Presbyterian church or Sunday school building.

In his last years Mr. Belk lost none of his mental vigor, nor did his sense of humor desert him. Invariably his eyes, bright and teasing in an otherwise impassive face, would betray him in his joking.

On a January 15 morning a year or two before his death, Mr. Belk was seated before his desk perusing the stores' reports when a reporter on the staff of one of the Charlotte newspapers entered his office.

The merchant swiveled around to face his guest, greeted

him cordially and then in all seriousness, as though he were addressing the president of the Chase National Bank, asked him:

"Could you let me have $186,000—today?"

The reporter, who would have been hard put to raise $186, saw the dancing eyes, answered just as soberly.

"But, Mr. Belk, that's a lot of money for me to get up on a day's notice. You ought to have asked me a couple of days ago. What do you want with the money anyway?"

The merchant was still unsmiling.

"It's time again to pay the Federal taxes, and they've got to be paid today."

"Well, I don't see how I can let you have the money— before tomorrow, at the earliest," the reporter answered. "What you going to do?"

"I've got the boys out scurrying around on the hunt for the money," he answered. "Hope they find it. I'd hate to go to jail."

A week later the reporter saw him again.

"Well, Mr. Belk, the boys must have got up that tax money," he said. "I see you're still out of jail."

This time he grinned wryly.

"Yes, they got it up," he said. "I was sure glad they found it."

W. H. BELK and his first grandchild, 1949

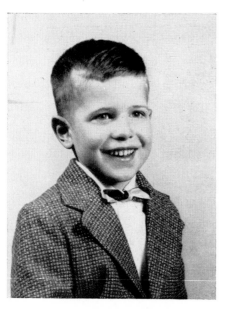

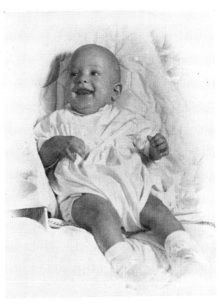

WILLIAM IRWIN BELK CARL GROTNES BELK

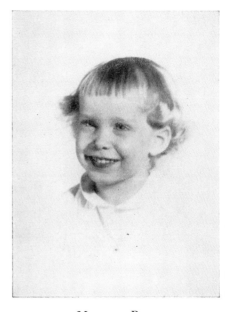

IRENE GROTNES BELK MARILYN BELK

CHILDREN OF IRWIN BELK

25

IN FEBRUARY, 1951, AFTER THE ANNUAL MEETINGS OF THE
stores' stockholders in his Charlotte office had been concluded, Mr. Belk went down to Florida to visit several of the
stores and particularly to stop again for a short while at his
orange grove at McIntosh, near Ocala.

He had owned the orange grove a long time and had taken
much interest in it, just as he had in his large farm holdings
in the section of the Waxhaws where he was born, though, as
he often pointed out, his farm operations had never shown
much profit. Nor had the orange grove produced him much

money, for most of the oranges had been given away to his friends at Christmas time.

Soon after his return from Florida, Mr. Belk developed influenza and was in the Presbyterian Hospital, next door to his home, for ten days. In April he underwent an operation there that kept him hospitalized several weeks, but by summertime he was able to begin coming again to his office for a short visit every other day.

On these trips to the office he was accompanied by his nurse, Miss Nora Welch of the Presbyterian Hospital's nursing staff. She wore her uniform and stayed close beside her patient. Very quickly she saw that even this small display of his illness was distressing Mr. Belk, so she tactfully changed into street dress for their visits to the office. Once they had arrived there, she left her patient under the watchful eyes of Miss Sarah Caddell, his secretary, until the time came for them to return to his home. Since his boyhood days Mr. Henry had been very much on his own, had forged his way, and now, nearing ninety, he was reluctant to picture himself an old man, dependent for physical aid upon someone else.

This characteristic attitude was even more strikingly revealed at the big Christmas party of the Buying Service office personnel late in December, 1951. Mr. Belk was able to attend. The party was being held in one of the large display rooms on the second floor. He had been brought along the corridor to his office in a wheel chair, and when the time arrived for him to go to the party, Miss Welch started wheeling him toward the elevator.

But Mr. Henry did not relish the thought of arriving at a Belk Christmas party—and invariably he had attended them in past years—in a wheel chair. So as they approached the elevator he ordered the wheel chair stopped. Slowly he climbed from the chair and erectly walked to the elevator. And he was walking when he joined the party.

It was his last one. Past the middle of February, however, he continued with more or less regularity to come down to the office. The weather now was very severe and Mr. Belk caught a heavy cold. On Tuesday, February 19, he became quite ill and began to experience difficulty in breathing. When it was found impossible that day to obtain a hospital room, an oxygen tent was set up on his own bed. Two days later when a room became available at Presbyterian Hospital, he was moved by ambulance the hundred yards and admitted.

That was in the early afternoon. Less than two hours later William Henry Belk was dead. The physicians said a heart attack had killed him. His tired body, worn all the more by the eight months of intermittent illness, had given way. He lacked less than four months of reaching his ninetieth birthday; he missed by more than five years attaining the age of his beloved mother.

John Belk was with the American forces in Korea, at the time on assignment in Japan, when his father died. The funeral was delayed in the hope that arrangements might be made for the son's return to Charlotte to attend it, but Captain Belk was unable to make the necessary flight connections and did not reach home until two weeks after his father's death.

The funeral was held on Sunday afternoon, February 24, at the Belk home on Hawthorne Lane. The officiating minister, the Reverend Charles G. McClure, D.D., pastor of Caldwell Memorial Presbyterian Church, had come to the Belk home from the funeral of one of Mr. Belk's long-time friends, the Reverend John G. Garth, Litt.D., held at the Reverend Mr. Garth's nearby home on Sunnyside Avenue.

It was a coincidence that the two were being laid to rest on the same Sunday afternoon. They had long been associated in various church activities. The minister for years had served as stated clerk of Mecklenburg Presbytery, the largest presbytery in the denomination. He and Mr. Belk had worked together on boards and commissions of that body and had joined efforts in the establishment of many new churches and the successful conclusion of various other philanthropic enterprises.

Henry Belk would have approved his funeral service. It was short and though impressive was without ostentation. Dr. McClure spoke briefly in tribute to Mr. Belk as a Christian churchman, a devoted family man, and an effective philanthropist, using as his theme the familiar lament of David on the death of Abner, "Know you not that there is a prince and a great man fallen this day in Israel?" The reading of a few verses from the Scriptures, a prayer, and the benediction concluded the service at the graveside in Charlotte's Elmwood cemetery.

A dignified though plain stone now stands at the head, a stone no more impressive than others about it. It marks the burial place of William Henry Belk, but it is not his memorial.

His memorials are in many places—alive and vigorous, producing dividends, dividends not only in material possessions but in the more lasting things of the spirit.

IX

THE MAN REMEMBERED

26

IN THE SEVERAL DAYS FOLLOWING THE DEATH OF MR. BELK many editorials in the newspapers of the Southeast, and in other sections of the nation, summarized the career of the Carolinas merchant and paid tribute to him as an able and far-seeing business leader, a devoted and effective churchman, and a generous contributor to many an important project.

Church publications also reviewed Mr. Belk's long life of achievement and joined with the secular press in developing the theme that "his record," as *The Charlotte Observer* commented, "has been a living proof that integrity of character, fortified by a firm religious faith, is the best foundation for achievement. . . ."

During the weeks following his death, many organizations —the National Retail Dry Goods Association, boards of directors of banks and other business enterprises, municipal governing groups, church courts, and other bodies—passed resolutions expressing their sorrow at the passing of the Carolinas mercantile leader, and countless letters of sympathy and condolence came to members of the family and associates in the management of the various stores.

None was more appreciated than the letter to Mrs. W. H. Belk and family from the men and women of Belk Brothers Company in Charlotte:

> The personnel of Belk Brothers Company wish to express some measure of our devotion to Mr. Belk and our deep sense of loss in his passing. This store is an institution which, like an individual, possesses a soul. Through the years Mr. Belk has built within it a spirit of honorable service, and through his genius each of us has caught a large vision of what a great business may be. From him we have learned that the poor man must be served as readily and as fully as the rich, and that only that store can succeed which remembers the dignity of the individual and considers its type of service a thing beyond mere profit taking.
>
> We are proud to have served under a generous-hearted man whose Christianity was apparent in his daily life. And we promise you our devoted efforts to keep this institution great, to make it an even more vital part of the community it serves.
>
> May you and your family find comfort in the knowledge that many people are glad that Mr. Belk lived.

That Mr. Belk had planned for the great merchandising empire he had founded to continue to be operated after his death very much in the manner of its operation in the years it was building was revealed with the reading of his will, recorded and proved March 1 in Mecklenburg Superior Court.

Under the terms of the will and two codicils, the widow and the six children inherited the bulk of the Belk estate. In the instrument Mr. Belk included the "fervent hope and prayer" that they and his "trusted business associates in the several Belk mercantile corporations" would continue to provide a "just and generous portion of the fruits thereof... for the advancement of Christian causes and the upbuilding of mankind."

The will provided for the setting up of trusts, with Mrs. Belk, the five sons and daughter, and A. F. Stevens of Winston-Salem, husband of a daughter of Dr. John M. Belk and long a close friend and business associate of Mr. Belk, as executors and trustees, to retain the existing plan of operation of the vast Belk mercantile enterprises.

The manner of operation is described in considerable detail in the document in elaboration of Mr. Belk's stated purpose to keep the several Belk corporations, then more than three hundred in number, operating under the family and business associates, rather than to liquidate any of the store properties and thereby convert such assets into money.

Mr. Belk envisioned that this plan, if carried out, would permit the continued functioning of the several Belk philanthropies, which throughout his long business career were foremost in his interest. To emphasize this interest and to urge the continuation of these philanthropic enterprises Mr. Belk set forth early in the will:

It is my fervent hope and prayer that after I have gone my sons and daughter and my trusted business associates in the several Belk mercantile corporations will use the properties in their charge and possession so that a just and generous portion of the fruits thereof, or part or parcel thereof, shall be used for the advancement of Christian causes and the upbuilding of mankind. I especially recommend

the Christian churches in the area in which the Belk mercantile corporations conduct their business, and particularly appropriate as
objects of Christian charity are small groups desiring to establish
new churches.

The John M. Belk Memorial Foundation has previously been established for the furtherance of such causes, and I commend this foundation to the continuing loyalty and charity of my family. It is my
request that at least once every five years at the regular annual
stockholders' meetings of the several Belk mercantile corporations,
so long as they remain in control of members of my family, the
language of this paragraph shall be read to the stockholders of said
corporations at such meetings. It is my hope and belief that with
the material blessings with which the Lord has blessed me and with
which the members of my family have been provided, they will see
fit to follow the good and charitable ways above set forth and
expressed.

The principal purposes of the John M. Belk Memorial
Foundation are: to aid groups of churches desiring to con-
struct new church edifices, principally in the Southeast, the
area in which there is the largest concentration of Belk stores;
to further the education and training of Christian workers
and missionaries to home and foreign fields; to establish and
aid public libraries; to aid hospitals and indigent patients;
to contribute to the support of Young Men's Christian Associations and Young Women's Christian Associations.

Two other foundations, one established shortly before Mr.
Belk's death, similar in nature and purpose to the John M.
Belk Foundation, had been set up by Mr. Belk and his associates to provide aid to charitable, educational, religious, cultural, and eleemosynary enterprises in which Mr. Belk long
had been interested.

Nothing perhaps would have given Henry Belk more satisfaction and delight than to have attended on May 29, 1954,
the laying of the cornerstone of a handsome building whose

cost had been financed in large part by the family and associates of Mr. Belk. The building, on the campus of Davidson College, an institution to which Mr. Belk was devoted and which for many years he had happily served as a trustee, bore his name. W. H. Belk Hall, one of the most modern college dormitories in North Carolina, was opened for use at the beginning of the fall term of 1955. It houses more than three hundred Davidson students.

Another honor, coveted perhaps by every American merchant who has achieved high success in his business career, had come to Mr. Belk the year following his death. On the occasion of the twenty-fifth anniversary, October 19-20, 1953, of the Boston Conference on Distribution, the Charlotte merchant was elected to the Hall of Fame in Distribution—a select list of men and women in distributing enterprises, including such leaders as Edward A. Filene and Lincoln Filene, Harvey S. Firestone, Jr., Elizabeth Arden, Bernard F. Gimbel, W. T. Grant, David Sarnoff, Helena Rubinstein, Jesse Isidor Straus, General Robert E. Wood, and others who have won fame and fortune in the business of selling.

The youth of the Waxhaw country who all his life had loved to trade and traffic had attained recognition as a merchant of world stature.

APPENDIX
CHRONOLOGICAL LIST OF
BELK STORES
AND
INDEX

APPENDIX

THE CHARLOTTE NEWS, FEBRUARY 22, 1952

In 1888, a tall, ramrod-straight young man with faith in the future and confidence in his own ability borrowed $500 at 10 per cent interest, added to it, $750 in personal savings, rented a building for $25 a month, and opened a drygoods store in Monroe. In six months he had repaid the loan and showed a clear profit of $3,300.

From that modest beginning, William Henry Belk rose to head the affairs of 306 Belk stores in fourteen states, and to direct the destinies of the many thousands who worked in them.

With the genius of merchandising, Mr. Belk was superbly equipped. His formula was relatively simple: sell good merchandise and, wherever possible, sell it for less. But to that formula he added other ingredients: handsome buildings and fixtures, attractive display, compelling advertising, and service to customers.

Even after he reached advanced years, Mr. Belk gave close personal attention to his business affairs. He did not need to. He had experienced managers and willing sons to carry the burden, but having been so integral a part of the merchandising empire for so long, he could not have given up his charge without feeling completely lost.

But William Henry Belk will also be remembered for other

things. A loyal churchman, he contributed to the building of hundreds of new churches over the whole South. And through his contributions to educational institutions, notably David-son and Queens Colleges, he helped provide the facilities and preserve the financial independence of private institutions of learning.

Reserved, dignified, retiring, Mr. Belk did not actively participate in public affairs. But he gave quiet and effective support to many worthwhile projects for building a better community here and in other places where Belk stores were situated.

His was a useful and productive life and its sudden termina-tion yesterday will cause genuine and widespread grief.

THE CHARLOTTE OBSERVER, FEBRUARY 23, 1952

If one were looking for a man whose life exemplifies the best in the American system and in American life, it would be hard to find a more apt illustration than the career of William Henry Belk, whose death Thursday left a vacant place that had seemed to be almost permanent in the life of Charlotte and of the South.

The record left behind him has been a living proof that integrity of character, fortified by a firm religious faith, is the best foundation for achievement in this land of ours. He built a mercantile empire that covered the whole Southeast, and he did it without benefit of RFC loans, aids to small business, or any other governmental favor. He started from scratch and rose at a time when the criterions for success were a man's ability, his will to achieve, his honesty of purpose.

Mr. Belk had all three in abundant measure. If there ever was a distress area, it was the South at the time he opened his first store. This region was in a desperate struggle to find its way out of the wreckage of a whole social and economic sys-

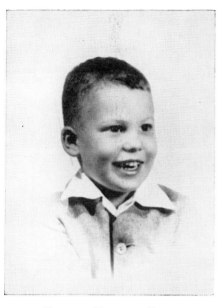

THOMAS EVERETT BELK

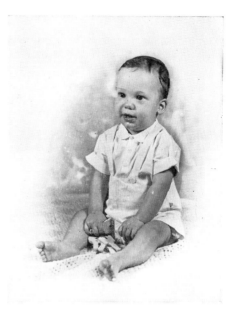

JAMES HERSCHEL BELK

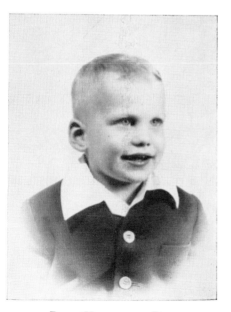

PAUL HENDERSON BELK

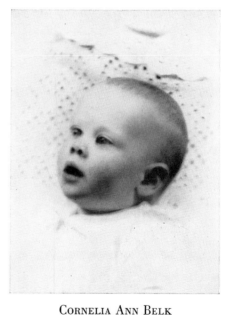

CORNELIA ANN BELK

CHILDREN OF HENDERSON BELK

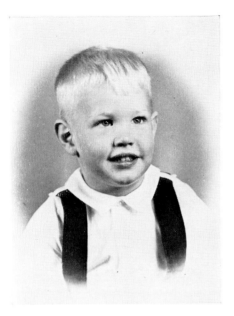

HAMILTON WITHERSPOON MCKAY BELK

JOHN ROBERT BELK

THOMAS MILBURN BELK, JR.

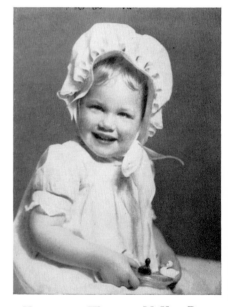

KATHERINE WHITNER MCKAY BELK

CHILDREN OF THOMAS M. BELK

tem. State governments were insolvent; private business was bankrupt; credit was almost unobtainable. In addition to all its other troubles, the South had dumped in its weary lap four million displaced persons that somehow had to be kept from starving.

We have seen no such distress area in our time. But there were no government contracts to be shunted to the South, no unemployment benefits for those four millions or their white friends, no public relief system, no aid to the aged or for dependent children, no price supports, no PWA, no CCC, no farm mortgage insurance, not even any organized markets for agricultural products.

It took a bold spirit to enter business under such circumstances with prospects for none but impoverished customers. But Belk's store drew the customers by a simple formula that never fails: it gave them value for their money and fair and honest treatment.

It succeeded so well that Mr. Belk established another store, then another and another. As the South recovered and grew, the Belk enterprises grew with it until they became identified with a region that he found in ruins and left on the crest of a great upsurge of both economic and cultural development.

It takes much more than mere business acumen to arrive at that kind of success. It takes character embedded in the old fashioned virtues. Mr. Belk had these virtues, but he had also a deep religious feeling, and the two combined to give him a conscience that would not let him rest while there was suffering in the world that he could do anything to alleviate.

Quietly and without fanfare he gave of his means to those causes which could strike at the root of social and economic evils and eliminate them at the source. His philanthropies were many and will be remembered long after him.

But the finest of all his legacies is the example of his own life, full to overflowing with a certain steadfastness that serves as an anchor in this turbulent age.

THE NEWS AND OBSERVER, RALEIGH, FEBRUARY 23, 1952

The death of William Henry Belk at the age of 89 removes from the list of pioneer merchants a North Carolinian whose merchandising practices had a considerable effect on the business life of this State.

When the first Belk store was opened in Monroe in 1888, all stores depended upon their charge accounts for most of their revenue. This led to abuses in the form of crop liens for farmers who were unable to pay and to exorbitant rates of interest. The Belk store, however, inaugurated the novel system of requiring cash for all purchases. It was a major innovation.

Five years after the first store opened, a branch store was launched and this process was repeated through the years until now the chain consists of nearly 300 outlets. The growth of the stores is ample testimony to the business acumen of their founder.

William Henry Belk long ago began investing his great wealth in philanthropies, concentrating on the Presbyterian Church. The John M. Belk Memorial Fund is credited with helping establish 335 Presbyterian churches and manses.

GREENSBORO DAILY NEWS, FEBRUARY 24, 1952

North Carolina lost another link with a fast-dying pioneer past in the death of William Henry Belk of Charlotte.

This kindly builder of a merchandising empire in 14 states appeared on the North Carolina scene 89 years ago along with warfare and tragedy. He grew up with hard times; they, in turn, created the challenge of his life. Out of it he forged a merchant empire that was unique, constructive and enduring.

As his biographer LeGette Blythe notes, one of his most notable monuments was the Belk merchandising system itself which trains young men in business techniques and sends them out to pioneer on their own.

And Belk's did something else too.

"In a day when the South was in the depths of direct poverty and business was done on the credit system, the Belks pioneered in such innovations as an all-cash, small-profit business, with retail prices clearly marked and no haggling at the counter."

But the founder himself was more than a conventional merchant prince. He was a deeply religious, humble man of simple habits and high ideals. It would be hard to measure the benefits of his philanthropies. He symbolized the best in business character, and on that foundation his success was built.

In the Greensboro region—and in Greensboro itself since 1898—Belk's has been a symbol of good business management, of integrity and fidelity to the best merchandising practices. We join the members of Mr. Belk's family, the 15,000 citizens who make up the lifeblood of the Belk empire and his many friends in mourning his passing.

THE HIGH POINT ENTERPRISE, FEBRUARY 23, 1952

"He was a great merchant" probably will be the public's first reaction to the death of William Henry Belk, 89, in Charlotte yesterday. And of course he was. A man who built and headed a chain of some 300 department stores in 14 states was a very great merchant. But the first reaction of those who knew him best probably will not concern his material success.

"He was a fine man" will be the statement of those who knew how William Henry Belk strove successfully to develop men at the same time he was developing stores; and those who knew of his benefactions, especially to churches.

We were somewhat surprised to read in the news story concerning his death that financial authorities considered William Henry Belk North Carolina's richest citizen. We didn't know he had accumulated so much money. But in another form of riches—the wealth which comes from a long life of many obstacles overcome, many tasks accomplished, many men helped and many good deeds done, William Henry Belk was even richer than he was in money.

THE MORNING HERALD, DURHAM, FEBRUARY 23, 1952

William Henry Belk, who died Thursday in Charlotte, belongs to the select company of industrialists and business leaders who were builders of the New South. He was among the last of a notable generation of men who refused to permit the environment of postwar poverty to shackle their lives and who literally forged out of hard times opportunity for themselves and for their fellows.

Mr. Belk brought to his business sound principles in relation both to his customers and his employees. The extent of the mercantile empire with which his name is connected is due to the application of these principles. By taking into partnership men of ability and giving them responsibility for management, he encouraged them to expand the Belk chain by opening new stores in new territory. By applying the sound principle of shrewd buying of merchandise, of offering for sale value at prices attractive to the bulk of the public, and by convincing advertising, Mr. Belk has given to the chain of stores with which he was associated a solid foundation in customer relations.

The passing of W. H. Belk removes one of North Carolina's great citizens. He was great because of his vision, because of his willingness to experiment in his mercantile business, because of his confidence in his associates, because of his willingness to experiment which he possessed and demonstrated.

THE DAILY RECORD, HICKORY, FEBRUARY 22, 1952

The passing in Charlotte of William Henry Belk, in his ninetieth year, recalls to Hickory area residents that this extraordinary man projected his influence into cities and towns throughout the entire Southeast.

Starting with a small drygoods store in Monroe in 1888, Mr. Belk soon demonstrated unusual business ability. By the time the present Belk-Broome Department Store was established in Hickory in 1920, the Belk Brothers chain already consisted of twenty-five stores. Today, with the passing of the founder, there are three hundred and five stores in fourteen states.

Karl W. Broome, who has been identified with the Hickory store ever since its establishment, has been one of the aggressive merchants of the Belk organization, and the fact that he and Mr. Belk added a half dozen stores under their combined name supplies an excellent example of how the parent company has expanded over such a wide expanse of territory.

Mr. Belk proved his interest in the Hickory area in many ways. For some years he served as president of Quaker Meadows Mills, located at Hildebran. He has also been identified with the Henry River Mills. In cooperation with Mr. Broome he sponsored the Belk Memorial Presbyterian church in Brookford and the Sweetwater Presbyterian church in East Hickory. In all, Mr. Belk helped establish more than 300 Presbyterian churches. He contributed liberally to projects for the development of better dairy stock, and has helped promote many worthy causes.

The W. H. Belk philanthropies included large gifts to

Davidson and Queens Colleges, erection of a seven-story building at Presbyterian Hospital in Charlotte, gifts to Presbyterian Junior College, and financial assistance to the program at Montreat.

He was one of the great merchants of our era, and like the Master whom he tried to emulate, he went about doing good to the end of his worldly career.

THE JOURNAL, WINSTON-SALEM, FEBRUARY 23, 1952

The death of W. H. Belk, founder of the Belk Brothers Company, focuses new attention upon the "better mousetrap" idea.

Mr. Belk pioneered in the "chain store-plus" program under which home-town men in each town where a Belk store was established became investing active partners in the business. This not only afforded additional capital for the Belk enterprises but also served to tie the stores more closely to the life and economy of the communities wherein they operated. Thus, in most of the scores of Southern towns and cities where there is a unit of the large chain this unit is not merely a "Belk Department Store," it is a "Belk-Stevens," a "Belk-Broome," a "Belk-Doughton" store, etc.

Mr. Belk, throughout his long lifetime—he was 89 when death overtook him this week—was a generous benefactor of churches, hospitals and schools. He took a keen and active interest in the progress and development of Charlotte, his adopted home community, the state and the Southeast.

But above and beyond his philanthropy Mr. Belk will be remembered for his genius as a merchant, his unshakable integrity as a business man and individual, and his simple unyielding faith in his fellows—a faith which enabled him to draw many brilliant young men into his organization and expand it into one of the nation's greatest mercantile empires.

THE INDEPENDENT, ANDERSON, S. C., FEBRUARY 23, 1952

The life span of William Henry Belk, the great Southern business man who died at the age of 89 in Charlotte, covered a period from the War Between the States to the Atomic Age.

As a child during the Civil War and as a youth during the Reconstruction Period, Mr. Belk knew first hand the hardship and the terror that were part of Southern living in these awful times.

He lived through other periods, too, when the South and the nation were buffeted by economic storms, when doubt and confusion rode the high winds, and many a man's faith failed.

From the time he took his first job in 1876 at the age of 14, he practiced the two virtues—hard work and Christian living —that were to take him to the pinnacle of success in this world and assure him of an honored place in the next.

Mr. Belk was a great salesman. He was also a believer in dealing squarely with his fellow man. Upon that foundation he built more than 300 stores throughout the Southeast. They are a monument to his business acumen, imagination, and courage.

When he was 87 years of age, somebody asked him if he expected ever to retire. "What would I want to retire for?" he asked. "I'm not overworked, I reckon. I like to stay busy. You know, I still like to sell things. I reckon I will as long as I live."

Despite his advanced age, Mr. Belk's death came as a shock to his associates. His long associate and friend in Anderson, W. Erskine Gallant, remarked that only a few days ago Mr. Belk sat in for awhile at a policy meeting in Charlotte.

One of the builders of our new and thriving South, Mr. Belk was keenly interested throughout his life in the work of the churches and connected institutions. How much money he gave in this direction is not known, but the amount is enormous.

In Anderson we are proud to have a church named in his honor, the Henry Belk Presbyterian Church in Homeland Park.

A great and good man has gone from us. His was an exemplary career, and any young man who should pattern his own life upon it could never go wrong.

THE STATE MAGAZINE, RALEIGH, NOVEMBER 1, 1952

When you write—or read—a success story of this nature there's one question that probably pops into everyone's mind: "What was the chief factor responsible for it?"

We've been giving this some thought and are inclined to believe that the answer is contained in one word—Character.

When the Belk brothers started their operations they did so on the basis (as quoted by Mr. Henry) that honesty is not only the best policy; it's the *only* policy. That was the cornerstone on which the business was founded, and it's the cornerstone of the business today. . . .

It's a tremendous achievement to have built up such a huge business organization: it's an even greater achievement to have done it on the basis of steadfast honesty and integrity that undoubtedly will continue for generations to come as present owners pass out of the picture and are succeeded by younger men who, too, have been trained the Belk way.

William Henry Belk has passed away, but it can truthfully be said that the greater part of him still lives and will continue to live.

THE MECKLENBURG PRESBYTERIAN, MARCH, 1952

"In Loving Appreciation and Cherished Memory of the Greatest Friend the Southern Presbyterian Church Ever Had" was engraved on a sterling silver plate to accompany the floral

Church design sent as a token of love and esteem from Mecklenburg Presbytery.

"He ... yet speaketh" is what the writer to the Hebrews said of Abel as he thought of his more excellent gift. It had been a long time—many, many generations—still it was said by an inspired writer—"He ... yet speaketh."

How appropriate of Mr. Belk—"He ... yet speaketh" from the hundreds of churches he has helped to build. Many of those churches were first in his planning. No one connected with his family or his great mercantile empire knows the extent of his philanthropies to churches.

"He yet speaketh" through three colleges in which he was deeply interested: Davidson, where a modern dormitory will bear his name; Presbyterian Junior College, of which he was a cofounder and to which he gave liberally to endowment and current expenses; Queens, whose campus has the lovely classic Greek Belk Chapel, given by the Belk interests in honor of the two great merchant princes—the other being Dr. John M. Belk, a brother.

"He yet speaketh" through great hospitals into which he has put thousands of dollars: The Presbyterian Hospital and the Sarah Walkup Hospital in Tai-Chow, China. In the latter institution, as in many others, there was the association of his like-minded brother, Dr. J. M. Belk, whose memory was always a precious and fragrant one. The hospital in China was built and equipped as a memorial to their mother.

"He yet speaketh" through the many people he has helped to educate: through the multitudes whose lives are richer and fuller and stronger because of the impact of his influence on them; through the now stalwart characters whom he discovered and gave a chance in life.

"He yet speaketh" through the thousands of Catechism awards—one dollar for reciting the Child's Catechism and two dollars for the Shorter. Mr. Belk knew that Calvinism made character and that the cream of Calvinism in the Catechisms was a good diet for young and old. The Catechisms in his thinking helped to lay moral and Christian foundations for one's life.

"He yet speaketh" through the more than three hundred stores that have his name. He has been acclaimed the world's greatest merchant.

"He yet speaketh" through his family, where there is such love and esteem. It is their plan to continue his plans as well as bear their own testimony to what is vital. He had the greatest love for his immediate family and those connected through ties of blood and marriage.

Mr. Belk's life began less than six months after the birth of the Southern Presbyterian Church in Augusta, Ga. They have lived and grown great together. His voice has not thundered from scores of pulpits. He has not sought the acclaim of the Church courts. But our Church never had a better friend or supporting member. It can be said without fear of contradiction that no one ever gave so much money to so many Southern Presbyterian institutions. Our Church is much larger and stronger today because of his statesmanlike vision. He would rather witness the organization of a new Presbyterian Sunday School, Chapel or Church than to know of the opening of a new Belk merchandising outlet. Home missions on any level would not be what it is except for his contribution in thought and finance. Montreat and the William Black Home have likewise been recipients of his generosity.

He had a real concern for the souls of men. His friendships were among all ages and classes. . . .

Mild mannered, soft spoken, courage of a lion but gentle as a lady, devotion to family and friends, the zeal of Paul, a double portion of the foundation grace of humility, much of the compassion of our Lord, God's good man—Dr. W. H. Belk—will be speaking for generations to come.

JOSH HORNE IN THE EVENING TELEGRAM,
ROCKY MOUNT, APRIL 3, 1952

A summarization of a life, in an expression of appreciation for kindnesses on the occasion of its passing, is a difficult undertaking. But within our judgment, we have never seen it better done than in the instance of the late William Henry Belk, the president of the Belk stores and head of the Belk-Tyler organization here, who slipped quietly from life's stage on February 21.

"Mr. Henry," as he was best known to those closest to him, has built a great mercantile empire but he never lost the human touch—was ever mindful of his church and its needs and he counted for much in the building of a greater and a better Southland. But the Belk family in five sentences expressed thanks for a long and useful life when they sent this expression to their friends. And we quote:

"The humble, devoted life that ever surrounded William Henry Belk was quietly stilled on the afternoon of February the 21st, 1952. Those who knew him well for nearly ninety years must share our feelings and comfort in Jesus' words, 'I am the resurrection and the life; he that believeth in me though he were dead, yet shall he live.' Though he has left our midst to join hands with the Father, his great faith and indomitable spirit ever challenge the best within us.

"Words fail us to tell how grateful we are for the love and sympathy expressed in so many ways in this time of our great bereavement. This has strengthened our faith and given us courage."

R. F. BEASLEY IN MONROE JOURNAL, MARCH 14, 1952

. . . When Mr. Belk died I felt another pillar that supported the world in which I grew up and one in which I had known so many stalwart figures, had fallen and further left the few remaining ones of us stranded. In the last paper I wrote in this column about Wade Hampton. The Civil War in which he took such a noble part ended a long era in American history and laid the way for a totally different one. In the midst of that conflict Mr. Belk was born and his father was one of its victims. His career epitomized the awful struggle which the South faced and he grew up in the wreckage, lived through it, knew it, never forgot it, but made a success so dazzling, and held so firmly to the ideals and principles which he inherited that his name, fame and work have become synonymous with the revitalized South and its glorious rise in a new and modern world.

. . . .

Though I knew Mr. Belk when as a youth he worked for Ben Heath, and for a period saw him each day as he hurried to his lunch at his mother's home where the Belk block now stands, I was never closely associated with him. That was because he went to Charlotte before I was grown and became active in the locality. But occasionally I saw him and he was always cordial and I am proud that he had this paper sent to his home in Charlotte as long as he lived and now and then wrote a note of appreciation. But I knew the Belk tradition so well that I felt I must know him perhaps better than some who were more closely associated with him in later years. I think that the greatest thing which can be said of a man who attains great success and especially great riches, is that such success never diverted him from the true course and solid foundations upon which his character and success were founded. Mr. Belk was a perfect example of this. Every act of his life ran true to form and as the maker and director of millions there was no flaw to mar his record. He never sought relaxation, entertainment or pleasure in the superficial life which so often traps the vanity of superficial men. The flies of night life never buzzed in his ears. On the contrary he sought and found satisfaction in the practice of the religious and human impulses in which he was born and reared. It has been said that the love of money is the root of all evil. Mr. Belk, maker of millions, had no such love. The accumulation of money wasn't his primary interest. Money was but a means of doing the work he loved, buying and selling, and expressing his goodwill, first to all those near and dear to him and then to others wherever they might be.

.   .   .   .

Abraham Lincoln said that God must have loved the common people because he made so many of them. Mr. Belk loved the common people because he understood and appreciated them. In their own school of adversity his character of self-denial, frugality, and helpfulness was formed. Though head of countless elegant stores and fine stocks in his later life, his first mercantile experience was with the people—all were then in that condition—who had little money and had to make every penny count. Because he made great efforts to meet their needs they came to his store and he never forgot what their friendship and patronage meant to him in the beginning years. And in his will which disposed of millions he provided that this attitude of his own life should continue to be preserved. Knowing his lifetime devotion to his mother, I feel sure that his life was founded upon his early association, friendship and love and understanding with her. Henry Belk was born pure gold, he died pure gold and his memory will be a fragrance to many people whose lives he touched.

Mr. Belk was an ornament to the soil from which he sprang and a knightly character in a new and commercial age which is sometimes thought to be a hard one. But as was said of

254   APPENDIX

Sir Galahad, "His strength was as the strength of ten because his heart was true."

RESOLUTION, BOARD OF TRUSTEES OF DAVIDSON COLLEGE

The world would call him a "merchant prince," because of his wise and successful business interests. Those who know him and his life recognize him as a princely Christian, personally devoted to our Lord and Saviour, bearing his likeness; like Paul a servant of Jesus Christ, in business for Christ, his real life's work and mission the promotion of Christ's saving cause and Kingdom.

To that end he gave himself personally to the service of his church, the Caldwell Memorial Presbyterian Church of Charlotte, in which he was an honored elder; and to Davidson College, of whose Board of Trustees he was a most interested and active member almost continuously since the year 1928, and which conferred upon him the degree of Doctor of Laws in recognition of his high achievements and true greatness of character, life, and service. To that end he was a faithful steward of Christ in the disposition of the material wealth that came into his hands, regarding himself as a trustee of Christ in the handling of his wealth. As such, he distributed this wealth here and there where it would accomplish the most in Christ's service: Gifts to hospitals, schools, colleges, to the building of churches and manses in many states, to missions and other benevolent causes.

His benefactions are too many to mention in this brief resolution. Indeed, many of them could not be mentioned for the reason that they are known only to him, the recipients, and his Lord. However, as the Board of Trustees of Davidson College, we do know and are most grateful for his many and large gifts to Davidson, which gifts at times led the way and made successful the campaigns of the College to secure funds for needed building expansion, the latest being a gift by the Belk family and associates of some $300,000 for the building of the William Henry Belk dormitory for the College. By such gifts to Christian education at Davidson and elsewhere, he revealed his recognition of such education as fundamental to the life and work of Christ's church and Kingdom.

In all sincerity we would point to Mr. Belk as the ideal Christian businessman, and pray to God to raise up others like him. Indeed, that very thing is the successful aim and endeavor of Davidson—to send forth from its walls Christian businessmen devoted to Christ, as well as men in the ministry and other professions.

To God who made and gave him is our gratitude for this one who helped so much to build Davidson of today. Our gratitude is also to this devoted and consecrated alumnus. Our sympathy is to his loved ones, from whose side he has been taken, whose consolation is that he has entered into the joy of his Lord and there awaits them.

CHILDREN AND GRANDCHILDREN OF MR. AND MRS.
WILLIAM HENRY BELK

William Henry Belk, Jr.—Married Phyllis Harper, January 27, 1950

> Their children: Mary Henry Belk, born October 27, 1951; died June 5, 1957
> William Henry Belk III, born February 23, 1953

Sarah Walkup Belk—Married Charles Glenn Gambrell, November 21, 1952

> Their child: Sarah Belk Gambrell, born March 17, 1960

John Montgomery Belk—Unmarried

Irwin Belk—Married Carol Grotnes, September 11, 1948

> Their children: William Irwin Belk, born August 21, 1949
> Irene Grotnes Belk, born June 28, 1950
> Marilyn Belk, born April 6, 1953
> Carl Grotnes Belk, born April 19, 1960

Henderson Belk—Married Ann Everett, June 10, 1949

> Their children: Thomas Everett Belk, born August 25, 1950
> Paul Henderson Belk, born November 27, 1952
> Cornelia Ann Belk, born July 22, 1954
> James Herschel Belk, born December 14, 1959

Thomas Milburn Belk—Married Katherine Whitner McKay, May 19, 1953

> Their children: Katherine Whitner McKay Belk, born February 28, 1954
> Thomas Milburn Belk, Jr., born March 17, 1955
> Hamilton W. McKay Belk, born January 24, 1957
> John Robert Belk, born February 4, 1959

Mr. and Mrs. W. H. BELK at the Henry Belk Presbyterian Church,
Anderson, South Carolina, which was built in honor of Mr. BELK

The W. H. BELK FAMILY, January, 1948, in front of the Belk home on Hawthorne Lane. *Left to right:* Henderson, William Henry, Jr., Irwin, Sarah, Mr. and Mrs. Belk, Tom, and John

WILLIAM HENRY BELK III   MARY HENRY BELK   SARAH BELK GAMBRELL

CHILDREN OF WILLIAM HENRY BELK, JR.

CHRONOLOGICAL LIST OF BELK STORES

Date Opened

December,	1926	Charleston, S. C.	Belk-Robinson Company
October,	1927	Lynchburg, Va.	Leggett's Department Store
December,	1927	Kinston, N. C.	Belk-Tyler Company
February,	1928	Smithfield, N. C.	Hudson-Belk Company
February,	1928	Johnson City, Tenn.	Parks-Belk Company
May,	1928	Mount Airy, N. C.	Belk's Department Store
May,	1928	North Wilkesboro, N. C.	Belk's Department Store
July,	1928	Rutherfordton, N. C.	Belk's Department Store
July,	1928	Lenoir, N. C.	Belk's Department Store
September,	1928	Spartanburg, S. C.	The Leader
November,	1928	Mooresville, N. C.	Belk's Department Store
November,	1928	South Boston, Va.	Leggett's Department Store
March,	1929	Oxford, N. C.	Leggett's Department Store
May,	1929	Winnsboro, S. C.	Belk's Department Store
July,	1929	Kingsport, Tenn.	Parks-Belk Company
November,	1929	Bristol, Va.	Parks-Belk Company
December,	1929	Elberton, Ga.	Gallant-Belk Company
December,	1929	Athens, Ga.	Gallant-Belk Company
February,	1930	Roxboro, N. C.	Leggett's Department Store
March,	1930	Lancaster, S. C.	Belk's Department Store
March,	1930	Greenville, S. C.	Belk-Simpson Suburban Department Store
June,	1930	Martinsville, Va.	Leggett's Department Store
June,	1930	Henderson, N. C.	Leggett's Department Store
August,	1930	High Point, N. C.	Belk-Stevens Company
September,	1930	Fayetteville, N. C.	Belk-Hensdale Company
September,	1930	Asheboro, N. C.	Hudson-Belk Company
November,	1930	Newberry, S. C.	Belk-Beard Company
December,	1930	Columbia, S. C.	Belk's Department Store
December,	1930	Lexington, N. C.	Belk-Martin Company
January,	1931	Morganton, N. C.	Belk-Broome Company
January,	1931	Greeneville, Tenn.	Parks-Belk Company
May,	1931	Orangeburg, S. C.	Belk-Hudson Company
June,	1931	Chatham, Va.	Leggett's Department Store
July,	1931	Elizabethton, Tenn.	Parks-Belk Company
August,	1931	Marion, N. C.	Belk-Broome Company
August,	1931	Roanoke Rapids, N. C.	Leggett's Department Store
October,	1931	Gaffney, S. C.	Belk's Department Store
November,	1931	Belmont, N. C.	Belk-Matthews Company
December,	1931	Galax, Va.	Belk's Department Store
		Canton, N. C.	Hudson's Department Store
September,	1932	Laurinburg, N. C.	Belk's Department Store
September,	1932	Morristown, Tenn.	Parks-Belk Company
October,	1932	Hartwell, Ga.	Gallant-Belk Company
November,	1932	Hamlet, N. C.	Belk's Department Store
March,	1933	Shelby, N. C.	Belk-Stevens Company
April,	1933	Kings Mountain, N. C.	Belk's Department Store

Date Opened

May,	1933	Suffolk, Va.	Leggett's Department Store
January,	1934	Goldsboro, N. C.	Belk-Tyler Company
March,	1934	Florence, S. C.	Belk's Department Store
April,	1934	New Bern, N. C.	Belk's Department Store
May,	1934	Lawrenceville, Va.	Leggett's Department Store
May,	1934	Gainesville, Ga.	Gallant-Belk Company
June,	1934	Rogersville, Tenn.	Parks-Belk Company
June,	1934	Greer, S. C.	The Leader
July,	1934	Griffin, Ga.	Belk-Gallant Company
July,	1934	Tarboro, N. C.	Belk-Tyler Company
August,	1934	Dunn, N. C.	Belk's Department Store
September,	1934	Laurens, S. C.	Belk's Department Store
September,	1934	Leaksville, N. C.	Belk-Cline Company
October,	1934	Abbeville, S. C.	Belk-Simpson Company
October,	1934	Marion, Va.	Parks-Belk Company
October,	1934	Radford, Va.	Leggett's Department Store
October,	1934	Altavista, Va.	Leggett's Department Store
October,	1934	Augusta, Ga.	Belk's Department Store
October,	1934	Pulaski, Va.	Parks-Belk Company
October,	1934	Monroe, Ga.	Gallant-Belk Company
October,	1934	Batesburg, S. C.	Belk-White Company
November,	1934	Winder, Ga.	Gallant-Belk Company
November,	1934	Sumter, S. C.	Belk-Stroman Company
	1934	Bedford, Va.	Leggett's Department Store
January,	1935	Thomasville, N. C.	Hudson-Belk Company
February,	1935	LaGrange, Ga.	Belk-Gallant Company
April,	1935	Newport News, Va.	Leggett's Department Store
April,	1935	Elizabeth City, N. C.	Belk-Tyler Company
April,	1935	Ocala, Fla.	Belk-Lindsey Company
May,	1935	Mullins, S. C.	Belk's Department Store
May,	1935	Dillon, S. C.	Belk's Department Store
May,	1935	Asheville, N. C.	Belk's Department Store
May,	1935	Asheville, N. C.	Fain's Thrift Store
May,	1935	Conway, S. C.	Belk's Department Store
May,	1935	Boone, N. C.	Belk's Department Store
July,	1935	Staunton, Va.	Leggett's Department Store
December,	1935	Camden, S. C.	Belk's Department Store
December,	1935	Clinton, S. C.	Belk's Department Store
December,	1935	Darlington, S. C.	Belk-Simpson Company
February,	1936	Lumberton, N. C.	Belk-Hensdale Company
February,	1936	Sparta, N. C.	Belk's Department Store
February,	1936	Forest City, N. C.	Belk-Logan Company
February,	1936	Hartsville, S. C.	Belk's Department Store
February,	1936	Valdese, N. C.	Belk-Broome Company
February,	1936	Cherryville, N. C.	Belk-Matthews Company
August,	1936	Covington, Va.	Leggett's Department Store
August,	1936	Franklin, Va.	Leggett's Department Store

Date Opened

October,	1936	Rome, Ga.	Belk-Rhodes Company
October,	1936	Anniston, Ala.	Hudson's Department Store
October,	1936	Washington, N. C.	Belk-Tyler Company
November,	1936	Chesterfield, S. C.	Belk's Department Store
December,	1936	Troy, N. C.	Belk-Cline Company
March,	1937	Walterboro, S. C.	Belk-Hudson Company
April,	1937	Brevard, N. C.	Belk's Department Store
April,	1937	Cleveland, Tenn.	Parks-Belk Company
May,	1937	West Jefferson, N. C.	Belk's Department Store
May,	1937	Williamston, N. C.	Belk-Tyler Company
May,	1937	Farmville, N. C.	Belk-Tyler Company
June,	1937	Woodruff, S. C.	Belk-Simpson Company
June,	1937	Christiansburg, Va.	Leggett's Department Store
July,	1937	McColl, S. C.	Belk's Department Store
July,	1937	Fort Mill, S. C.	Belk-Brown Company
August,	1937	Warrenton, N. C.	Leggett's Department Store
September,	1937	Toccoa, Ga.	Belk-Gallant Company
September,	1937	Whiteville, N. C.	Belk-Hensdale Company
September,	1937	Portsmouth, Va.	Leggett's Department Store
September,	1937	Ahoskie, N. C.	Belk-Tyler Company
September,	1937	Kershaw, S. C.	Belk-Hagins Company
September,	1937	Wilmington, N. C.	X Department Store
September,	1937	Albany, Ga.	Belk's Department Store
October,	1937	Gadsden, Ala.	Belk-Hudson Company
April,	1938	Elkin, N. C.	Belk-Doughton Company
July,	1938	Clarksville, Tenn.	Parks-Belk Company
September,	1938	Siler City, N. C.	Belk-Yates Company
October,	1938	Greenville, N. C.	Belk-Tyler Company
November,	1938	Bishopville, S. C.	Belk's Department Store
November,	1938	Honea Path, S. C.	Belk-Simpson Company
November,	1938	Ware Shoals, S. C.	Gallant-Belk Company
December,	1938	Spruce Pine, N. C.	Belk-Broome Company
December,	1938	Waynesville, N. C.	Belk-Hudson Company
January,	1939	Newport, Tenn.	Parks-Belk Company
February,	1939	Charlottesville, Va.	Leggett's Department Store
February,	1939	Clifton Forge, Va.	Leggett's Department Store
March,	1939	Columbia, S. C.	Howard's Department Store
March,	1939	Hendersonville, N. C.	Belk-Simpson Company
March,	1939	Marshall, N. C.	Belk-Broome Company
May,	1939	Louisburg, N. C.	Leggett's Department Store
September,	1939	Emporia, Va.	Leggett's Department Store
September,	1939	Seneca, S. C.	Gallant-Belk Company
September,	1939	Marion, S. C.	Belk's Department Store
November,	1939	Valdosta, Ga.	Belk-Hudson Company
November,	1939	Bryson City, N. C.	Belk's Department Store
December,	1939	Waynesboro, Va.	Leggett's Department Store
June,	1940	Madison, N. C.	Belk-Cline Company

Date Opened

November,	1940	Culpeper, Va.	Leggett's Department Store
November,	1940	Abingdon, Va.	Parks-Belk Company
November,	1940	Cornelia, Ga.	Belk-Gallant Company
December,	1940	Great Falls, S. C.	Belk's Department Store
February,	1941	Moultrie, Ga.	Belk-Hudson Company
February,	1941	Wytheville, Va.	Leggett's Department Store
April,	1941	Newnan, Ga.	Belk-Gallant Company
April,	1941	Huntsville, Ala.	Belk-Hudson Company
July,	1941	West Point, Ga.	Belk-Gallant Company
July,	1941	Gainesville, Fla.	Belk-Lindsey Company
October,	1941	Washington, Ga.	Belk-Gallant Company
December,	1941	Winchester, Va.	Leggett's Department Store
December,	1941	Dalton, Ga.	Belk-Gallant Company
May,	1942	Macon, Ga.	Belk-Matthews Company
June,	1942	Georgetown, S. C.	Belk-Scarboro Company
July,	1942	Decatur, Ala.	Belk-Hudson Company
September,	1942	Wilson, N. C.	Belk-Tyler Company
	1942	Kannapolis, N. C.	Belk's Bargain Store
January,	1943	Draper, N. C.	Belk-Cline Company
March,	1943	Sylva, N. C.	Belk's Department Store
June,	1943	Marysville, Tenn.	Parks-Belk Company
October,	1943	Leaksville, N. C.	Boulevard Store
October,	1943	Mount Gilead, N. C.	Belk-Cline Company
December,	1943	Fountain Inn, S. C.	The Putman Company
January,	1944	Beaufort, S. C.	Belk-Simpson Company
February,	1944	Walhalla, S. C.	Belk-Gallant Company
February,	1944	LaGrange, Ga.	B & G Bargain Store
August,	1944	Talladega, Ala.	Belk-Hudson Company
August,	1944	Commerce, Ga.	Belk-Gallant Company
August,	1944	Asheville, N. C.	B & J Department Store
September,	1944	Covington, Ga.	Belk-Gallant Company
October,	1944	Winter Haven, Fla.	Belk-Lindsey Company
December,	1944	Lawrenceville, Ga.	Belk-Gallant Company
February,	1945	Royston, Ga.	Gallant-Belk Company
March,	1945	Clayton, Ga.	Belk-Gallant Company
June,	1945	Raeford, N. C.	Belk-Hensdale Company
June,	1945	Fort Myers, Fla.	Belk-Lindsey Company
September,	1945	Edgefield, S. C.	Belk-Gallant Company
September,	1945	Timmonsville, S. C.	Belk's Department Store
October,	1945	Manning, S. C.	Belk-Simpson Company
October,	1945	Franklin, N. C.	Belk's Department Store
November,	1945	Jackson, N. C.	Leggett's Department Store
November,	1945	Winchester, Ky.	Belk-Simpson Company
April,	1946	Alexander City, Ala.	Belk-Hudson Company
April,	1946	Chase City, Va.	Leggett's Department Store
April,	1946	Dawson, Ga.	Belk-Hagins Company
April,	1946	Randleman, N. C.	Belk-Yates Company

Date Opened

May,	1946	Henderson, Ky.	Belk-Henderson Company
June,	1946	Mayfield, Ky.	Parks-Belk Company
June,	1946	Luray, Va.	Leggett's Department Store
July,	1946	Hartselle, Ala.	Belk-Hudson Company
August,	1946	Shelbyville, Tenn.	Parks-Belk Company
August,	1946	Victoria, Va.	Leggett's Department Store
August,	1946	Ironton, Ohio	Leggett's Department Store
August,	1946	Palatka, Fla.	Belk-Lindsey Company
September,	1946	Carrollton, Ga.	Belk-Rhodes Company
September,	1946	Cartersville, Ga.	Belk-Gallant Company
September,	1946	Farmville, Va.	Leggett's Department Store
September,	1946	Manchester, Ga.	Belk-Gallant Company
September,	1946	Red Springs, N. C.	Belk-Hensdale Company
September,	1946	Roanoke, Ala.	Belk-Gallant Company
September,	1946	Cambridge, Md.	Leggett's Department Store
September,	1946	Dublin, Ga.	Belk-Matthews Company
October,	1946	Savannah, Ga.	Belk's Department Store
October,	1946	Sheffield, Ala.	Belk-Hudson Company
October,	1946	Douglas, Ga.	Belk-Hudson Company
October,	1946	Murray, Ky.	Belk-Settle Company
October,	1946	Sylacauga, Ala.	Belk-Hudson Company
December,	1946	Hampton, Va.	Leggett's Department Store
December,	1946	Corinth, Miss.	Belk-Hudson Company
February,	1947	Mount Sterling, Ky.	Belk-Simpson Company
February,	1947	McMinnville, Tenn.	Parks-Belk Company
July,	1947	Orange, Va.	Leggett's Department Store
July,	1947	Aiken, S. C.	Belk's Department Store
August,	1947	Corbin, Ky.	Belk-Simpson Company
September,	1947	Hogansville, Ga.	Belk-Gallant Company
October,	1947	Clarksville, Ga.	Belk-Gallant Company
October,	1947	Texarkana, Ark.-Texas	Belk-Jones Company
November,	1947	Montgomery, Ala.	Belk-Matthews Company
November,	1947	Cairo, Ga.	Belk-Hudson Company
November,	1947	Bradenton, Fla.	Belk-Lindsey Company
February,	1948	Lake City, S. C.	Belk's Department Store
February,	1948	Greenville, Ala.	Belk-Hudson Company
May,	1948	Hattiesburg, Miss.	Belk-Croen Company
May,	1948	Lawrenceburg, Tenn.	Parks-Belk Company
May,	1948	Madison, Ga.	Gallant-Belk Company
June,	1948	Pensacola, Fla.	Belk-Hudson Company
August,	1948	Decatur, Ga.	Belk-Gallant Company
August,	1948	Robbins, N. C.	Belk-Cline Company
August,	1948	Tifton, Ga.	Belk-Hudson Company
October,	1948	Brookneal, Va.	Leggett's Department Store
December,	1948	Plant City, Fla.	Belk-Lindsey Company
February,	1949	Bainbridge, Ga.	Belk-Simpson Company

Date Opened		
March, 1949	China Grove, N. C.	Belk-Cline Company
March, 1949	Sandersville, Ga.	Belk-Gallant Company
March, 1949	Americus, Ga.	Belk's Department Store
April, 1949	Thomasville, Ga.	Belk's Department Store
August, 1949	Fuquay Springs, N. C.	Belk-Hudson Company
August, 1949	Kingstree, S. C.	Belk's Department Store
September, 1949	Edenton, N. C.	Belk-Tyler Company
September, 1949	Plymouth, N. C.	Belk-Tyler Company
December, 1949	Fort Lauderdale, Fla.	Belk-Lindsey Company
February, 1950	Fayetteville, N. C.	B & H Department Store
August, 1950	Pittsboro, N. C.	Belk-Yates-Beck Company
August, 1950	Statesboro, Ga.	Belk's Department Store
September, 1950	Gadsden, Ala.	Gadsden Thrift Store
September, 1950	Myrtle Beach, S. C.	Belk's Department Store
October, 1950	Leesburg, Fla.	Belk-Sawyer Company
February, 1951	Dade City, Fla.	Belk-Lindsey Company
March, 1951	West Point, Va.	Leggett's Department Store
March, 1951	Columbus, Miss.	Belk-Hudson Company
March, 1951	Granite Falls, N. C.	Belk-Broome Company
May, 1951	Camden, Ark.	Belk-Jones Company
May, 1951	Jacksonville, N. C.	Belk's Department Store
May, 1951	Elizabethtown, N. C.	Belk-Hensdale Company
August, 1951	Lewisburg, W. Va.	Leggett's Department Store
September, 1951	Morehead City, N. C.	Belk's Department Store
September, 1951	Cheraw, S. C.	Belk's Department Store
September, 1951	Milledgeville, Ga.	Belk-Matthews Company
September, 1951	Franklinton, N. C.	Leggett's Department Store
September, 1951	Tuscaloosa, Ala.	Belk-Hudson Company
October, 1951	Anniston, Ala.	Kitchin's Thrift Store
November, 1951	Charlottesville, Va.	Leggett's Bargain Center
November, 1951	Portsmouth, Va.	Leggett's Bargain Center
November, 1951	Belton, S. C.	Gallant-Belk Company
February, 1952	Mt. Olive, N. C.	Belk-Tyler Company
August, 1952	Weldon, N. C.	Leggett's Department Store
November, 1952	St. Petersburg, Fla.	Belk-Lindsey Company
January, 1953	Denison, Texas	Belk's Department Store
March, 1953	Atlanta (Buckhead), Ga.	Belk-Gallant Company
March, 1953	Charlotte, N. C.	The Bottom Dollar
March, 1953	Graham, N. C.	Belk-Beck Company
May, 1953	South Hill, Va.	Leggett's Department Store
July, 1953	Rocky Mount, Va.	Leggett's Department Store
August, 1953	Paris, Texas	Belk's Department Store
August, 1953	Wendell, N. C.	Hudson-Belk Company
August, 1953	Lynchburg, Va.	Leggett's Community Center
December, 1953	Lexington, Va.	Leggett's Department Store
March, 1954	Charleston, S. C.	Belk-Robinson Suburban

Date Opened

April,	1954	Fitzgerald, Ga.	Belk's Department Store
May,	1954	Cedartown, Ga.	Belk-Rhodes Company
August,	1954	Palestine, Texas	Belk's Department Store
August,	1954	Tampa, Fla.	Belk-Lindsey Company
October,	1954	West Palm Beach, Fla.	Belk's Department Store
October,	1954	Lake City, Fla.	Belk-Hudson Company
November,	1954	Paragould, Ark.	Belk-Simpson Company
November,	1954	Harlan, Ky.	Belk-Simpson Company
November,	1954	Athens, Ohio	Belk-Simpson Company
November,	1954	Carthage, Mo.	Belk-Simpson Company
February,	1955	Whitmire, S. C.	Belk-Simpson Company
February,	1955	Birmingham, Ala.	Belk-Hudson Company
April,	1955	Aberdeen, N. C.	Belk-Hensdale Company
April,	1955	Chapel Hill, N. C.	Belk-Leggett-Horton Company
May,	1955	Thomson, Ga.	Belk-Gallant Company
June,	1955	Princeton, W. Va.	Leggett's Department Store
June,	1955	Panama City, Fla.	Belk-Chastain Company
September,	1955	Savannah, Ga.	Belk-Griffeth Company
October,	1955	Memphis, Tenn.	Parks-Belk Company (Park Avenue)
February,	1956	Shelbyville, Ind.	Parks-Belk Company
March,	1956	Frankfort, Ky.	Belk-Simpson Company
March,	1956	Fredericksburg, Va.	Leggett's Department Store
April,	1956	Asheboro, N. C.	Yates Thrift Store
June,	1956	Atlanta, Ga.	Belk-Gallant Company (Campbellton Road)
August,	1956	Quincy, Fla.	Belk-Hudson Company
September,	1956	Monroe, La.	Belk-Gallant Company
November,	1956	Memphis, Tenn.	Parks-Belk (Summer Avenue)
May,	1957	Harrisonburg, Va.	Leggett's Department Store
July,	1957	Augusta, Ga.	Belk's Suburban Department Store
July,	1957	New Tazewell, Tenn.	Parks-Belk Company
August,	1957	Greensboro, N. C.	Belk's Suburban Department Store
November,	1957	Bluefield, W. Va.	Leggett's Department Store
November,	1957	West Point, Miss.	Belk-Hudson Company
March,	1958	Vidalia, Ga.	Belk-Matthews Company
July,	1958	Stuttgart, Ark.	Belk-Jones Company
September,	1958	Warner Robins, Ga.	Belk-Matthews Company
October,	1958	Danville, Ky.	Parks-Belk Company
September,	1959	Rome, Ga.	Rome Thrift Store
September,	1959	Charleston, S. C.	Belk-Robinson Company (Pinehaven Shopg. Ctr.)

Date Opened

November,	1959	Jefferson City, Tenn.	Parks-Belk Company
March,	1960	Thomaston, Ga.	Belk-Gallant Company
March,	1960	Pearisburg, Va.	Leggett's Department Store
April,	1960	Charles Town, W. Va.	Leggett's Department Store
September,	1956	Concord, N. C.	Efird's Department Store
September,	1956	Gastonia, N. C.	The Efird Company
September,	1956	Rock Hill, S. C.	Efird's Department Store
September,	1956	Anderson, S. C.	Efird's Department Store
September,	1956	Greenville, S. C.	The Dollar Store
September,	1956	Greenwood, S. C.	Efird's Department Store
September,	1956	Spartanburg, S. C.	Efird's Department Store
September,	1956	Lenoir, N. C.	Efird's Department Store
September,	1956	Statesville, N. C.	Efird's Department Store
September,	1956	Wilmington, N. C.	Efird's Department Store
September,	1956	Albemarle, N. C.	Efird's Department Store (John E. Efird & Sons)
September,	1956	Florence, S. C.	Efird's Department Store
September,	1956	Chester, S. C.	Efird's Department Store
September,	1956	Asheville, N. C.	Efird's Department Store
September,	1956	Charleston, S. C.	Efird's Department Store
September,	1956	Sanford, N. C.	Efird's Department Store
September,	1956	Smithfield, N. C.	Efird's Department Store
September,	1956	Thomasville, N. C.	Efird's Department Store
February,	1959	Clinton, S. C.	Efird's Department Store
May,	1960	Miami (Coral Gables, Fla.)	Belk's Department Store (5741 Bird Rd. SW)
May,	1960	Ybor City, Tampa, Fla.	Belk-Lindsey Company
May,	1960	Largo, Fla.	Belk-Lindsey Company
May,	1960	Sarasota, Fla.	Belk-Lindsey Company
May,	1960	Orlando, Fla.	Belk-Lindsey Company (Colonial Plaza)
May,	1960	Punta Gorda, Fla.	Belk-Lindsey Company
May,	1960	Tampa, Fla.	Belk-Lindsey Company (Armenia)
May,	1960	Titusville, Fla.	Belk-Lindsey Company
May,	1960	Melbourne, Fla.	Belk-Lindsey Company
May,	1960	Cocoa, Fla.	Belk-Lindsey Company
May,	1960	Bayamon, Puerto Rico	Belk-Lindsey Company
May,	1960	Daytona Beach, Fla.	Belk-Lindsey Company
June,	1960	Paris, Tennessee	Belk-Settle Company
June,	1960	Union City, Tenn.	Belk-Settle Company
August,	1960	London, Ky.	Parks-Belk Company
August,	1960	St. Petersburg, Fla.	Wm. Henry, Inc.
August,	1960	Miami, Fla.	Belk-Lindsey Company (79th & Biscayne)

Date Opened

August,	1960	Miami Beach, Fla.	Belk-Lindsay Co. (Sunny Isles)
October,	1960	Decatur, Ga.	Belk-Gallant Suburban (N. Decatur Rd.)
October,	1960	Forest Park, Ga.	Belk-Gallant Company
November,	1960	Bluefield, W. Va.	Leggett's, Inc. (200 Federal St.)
January,	1961	Tampa, Fla. (Britton Plaza)	Belk-Lindsey Co.

INDEX